DIAMONDFIELD JACK
A Study in Frontier Justice

Date Due

Diamondfield Jack, a free man in the boomtown of Tonopah, Nevada, 1903. (Courtesy of Nell Murbarger)

Diamondfield Jack

A Study in Frontier Justice

BY DAVID H. GROVER, 1925-

UNIVERSITY OF OKLAHOMA PRESS
NORMAN AND LONDON

Library of Congress Cataloging-in-Publication Data

Grover, David H. (David Hubert), 1925-
  Diamondfield Jack: a study in frontier justice.

  Bibliography, p.
  Includes index.
  1. Davis, Jackson Lee, 1870?-1949—Trials, litigation,
etc. 2. Trials (Murder)—Idaho—Cassia County. 3. Cassia
County (Idaho)—History. I. Title.
KF223.D5G7   1986   345.73'02523   85-40940
ISBN 0-8061-1979-9   347.3052523

*To Marilyn, a wife whose talents
lie in being a woman,
not an editorial assistant—
an arrangement for which
the author is forever grateful.*

Contents

Illustrations

Preface to the Paperback Edition

IT IS always gratifying to an author when one of his or her books is given a new lease on life. To this author it is particularly gratifying that Diamondfield Jack will be around a while longer inasmuch as the gunman-turned-goldminer, in spite of his faults, has taken on the status of an old friend—even though we never met.

Jack Davis originally came into my life completely by accident. His name appeared in some leftover notes that I retained after completing my first book, which dealt with the Haywood trial in Boise in 1907. Those notes alluded to another great legal battle in Idaho which also involved the Haywood trial attorneys, James H. Hawley and William E. Borah, a murder case growing out of a cattle-sheep war in the 1890's. The defendant in that trial was the man known as Diamondfield Jack Davis. Initially there was no compelling reason to try a book on what appeared to be only an incident in local history. The decision to write the book on this case came only after Merle Wells, the director of the Idaho Historical Society, told me, "Now, there's the case that really needs a book written about it."

In the years since this book was first published, I have continued to have warm feelings about the man whom I helped to introduce to readers of western history. Editors and reviewers also seem to have liked Diamondfield Jack, perhaps because he talked such a good line as an archetypal hired gunman but actually behaved as a relatively mild and harmless man. In that combination of traits there is something inherently appealing, almost theatrical.

The dramatic elements of the man and his story have since been exploited in other media and other formats. In the early 1970's a little theater group in Idaho put together a dramatic production of the Diamondfield Jack story. In the middle of that decade Cactus Pete's casino in Jackpot, Nevada, near the site of the old Boar's Nest ranch of the Sparks-Harrell empire, staged an annual competitive trail ride for several years as a reenactment of the fifty-five-mile ride Diamondfield Jack would have had to make to kill the sheepherders. Jackpot, now a pleasant resort complex and perhaps the most attractive of Nevada's stateline gambling communities, has both enhanced and benefited from the Diamondfield Jack legend. There, after one of the trail rides, the author met the young country-western musician Frank Farah and heard him sing to a casino audience a ballad about Diamondfield Jack which he had recently written and recorded.

Through the ensuing years it has been somewhat surprising that Hollywood apparently has not discovered and exploited Jack Davis. Perhaps this neglect reflects an awareness that no genre of western film exists which could properly accommodate in a central role the unusual and contradictory elements of his character: villainy and honor, bravado and courage, talk and action, lies and candor. Such a personality might more readily be treated in a musical than through the realism of film; it is not hard to imagine a Gilbert and Sullivan version of Diamondfield Jack as the very model of a cattle-company gunman who fights a range war with talk, is always gunning for a sheep-man who does not seem to be on the range that day, who believes in "cutting it in smoke" for the honor of it, but who cannot ride hard because of a painful dose of a venereal disease.

In a more serious vein, one of the most difficult things to understand about Diamondfield Jack is how, after his incredible reversal of fortune in Nevada, he was unable to hang onto the wealth, power, and quasirespectability he had acquired. After struggling with only limited success to answer this question, the author has concluded that it would have been out of character for Diamondfield Jack to have become a conventional success. He seemed destined always to be a loner, perhaps even a star-crossed loser, one of that breed described romantically by the poet Robert W. Service as "the men who don't fit in."

The author agrees with those critics and reviewers who felt that additional information and interpretation would have been useful at several points in the telling of the Diamondfield Jack story. Unfortunately, that material simply was not available. Nor has any new evidence sur-faced since the time the book was originally published that would answer remaining questions or materially change any of the findings. We may have learned from the Jackpot trail rides (which were eventually terminated after the Bureau of Land Management objected to the large number of riders thundering across the sagebrush) that the fifty-five-mile ride could have been made in a lot less than five hours, but we have no more reason to be-lieve that Diamondfield Jack made the ride than we did earlier. We know something more of Davis's role as a key law-and-order figure during the Goldfield labor troubles (and conceivably we may learn more when the date arrives for the opening of the George Wingfield papers at the Nevada Historical Society), but we know nothing more of his early life and only a little more of his later career as a mining man. Furthermore, our chances to learn anything more may be slipping away.

As a rule, historians do not lament the passing of an era; after all, the passage of time is the basic raw material of history. What they do regret, however, is the passing of a follow-up period during which younger contemporaries of the interesting figures of the earlier era are still alive and can contribute to the oral history of the era. For Diamondfield Jack that follow-up period has now ended. In the two decades that have passed since the author first began to explore this case, all of Davis's contemporaries who could have told us more about the man, his work, and his times have themselves passed from the scene. Although the author talked to a few such people early in the 1960's, indeed all that he could locate, he is now aware that he missed others whom he wishes he could have found. Now that they are all gone, it is natural to feel a twinge of regret.

But, on balance, there are no real regrets in seeing this turn-of-the-century affair fade further into the distance. As we approach another turn-of-the-century we are reminded that while Diamondfield Jack's generation is no longer within our direct reach, a new generation of readers and history buffs *is*. Inasmuch as a book is an introductory link between generations, the continued presence of this book means that Diamondfield Jack is still around for those who would like to know him better.

DAVID H. GROVER

Napa, California

xiv

Acknowledgments

THE RESEARCH for this book was carried out under grants from Oregon State University and Colorado State University. The resources of the following libraries were particularly useful: Oregon State University, University of Oregon, University of Colorado, Colorado State University, University of Nevada, Nevada Southern University, University of Wyoming, The Bancroft Library of the University of California, the New York Public Library, the Library of Congress, the Western History collection of the Denver Public Library, and the Nevada State Library.

The author gratefully acknowledges the help of the following historical agencies: Idaho Historical Society, Nevada Historical Society, Southern Nevada Historical Society, Utah State Historical Society, Tulare County Historical Society, National Cowboy Hall of Fame, and the Historian of the Church of Jesus Christ of Latter Day Saints.

The following individuals were particularly helpful:

Mrs. Myrtle Myles of Reno, Nevada; Mrs. Velma Stevens Truett of Elko, Nevada; Victor Goodwin of Carson City, Nevada; Frank Kearns, Clerk of Cassia County, Idaho; Louis Bidaganeta, Clerk of the Idaho Supreme Court; Frank Jordan, California Secretary of State; Yvonne Peattie of Los Angeles; Mrs. Celesta Lowe of Tecopa, California; Mrs. Margaret A. Peterson of Seattle, Washington.

Two corporations were helpful in locating information: the Tidewater Oil Company of Los Angeles and the J. R. Simplot Company of Boise, Idaho.

D.H.G.

DIAMONDFIELD JACK
A Study in Frontier Justice

An Introduction to the Diamondfield Jack Affair

IN THE SUMMER of 1895 a swaggering young cowboy hired out to the Sparks-Harrell Cattle Company to ride the ranges of southern Idaho. It was a fateful decision that was soon to bring grief to all whom it touched, bitter conflict to the area, the loss of great amounts of money and prestige to the cattle company, and a date with the hangman for the cowboy—Diamondfield Jack Davis.

Through the next seven years evolved one of the strangest legal dramas of western America—the Diamondfield Jack case. What began as an isolated rangeland shooting became, in the course of time, the focal point of a long and bitter court fight between powerful and wealthy livestock interests, a political controversy that divided public opinion throughout Idaho, and even at times a quasi-religious issue which fanned the dying embers of anti-Mormonism.

In the more than sixty years since that time a number of writers have made fleeting references to the more spectacular events of the long legal battle, but most accounts have been inaccurate and incomplete. As a result, misconceptions and prejudices about the case still exist. This book is an attempt to set the record straight —to examine objectively and dispassionately the facts of the case, and perhaps to offer an explanation of why things happened the way they did.

The story is woven together from the many threads that exist independently in court records, newspaper stories, correspondence, depositions, and statements of Idaho and Nevada people. Because of the large number of nondescript legal documents and letters involved, no attempt has been made to cite in conventional footnote form the exact source for certain facts. Instead, most notes refer only to the general location of documentation, which is preserved primarily in the voluminous Hawley papers of the Idaho Historical Society.

Much credit should go to the Idaho Historical Society in Boise for collecting these important primary source materials, and to the Nevada Historical Society in Reno for documenting certain aspects of the later life of Diamondfield Jack. There are "loose ends" in this story, to be sure—facts which simply do not fit into place properly—but this condition exists in the analysis of any great episode of crime and punishment, serving to heighten the intrigue and human interest.

The Diamondfield Jack affair is complex. In the pages that follow, several facets of the affair are explored simultaneously: the narrative account of a dramatic western shooting and its aftermath, a complicated case in law that was eventually considered by the Supreme

Court, and an episode in regional history with widespread personal entanglements. But primarily the Diamondfield Jack affair is a study of people—of cattle barons and cowboys, sheepmen and sheepherders, lawyers and newspapermen—caught up in a strange web of circumstances and emotionalism. In the role of hero or villain was the garrulous Diamondfield Jack Davis, a man who talked his way into more trouble in a few short years than most people encounter in a lifetime. Although he never had the lasting notoriety of his more celebrated contemporaries—Tom Horn, Butch Cassidy, and the other gunmen of the closing days of the frontier—Diamondfield Jack in all respects played his role as convincingly as the others.

If it is possible for a man to be "a legend in his own time," then Diamondfield Jack must be accorded this distinction. He was the nefarious cowboy gunman about whom this book is written, and in later years the mysterious rags-to-riches mining man whose far-ranging activities will probably never be fully known. This, then, is the story of Jackson Lee Davis, alias Diamondfield Jack.

Chroniclers consider this rare portrait of Diamondfield Jack as highly revealing of his character. (From *Western World,* April, 1905; courtesy of Denver Public Library Western Collection)

II

Diamondfield Jack, the Garrulous Gunman

In most respects, Jack Davis looked like an ordinary young cowboy. He had the ruddy face of an outdoorsman, deep-set grey eyes, dark hair, and a sandy mustache. He was neither tall nor imposing—standing only five feet seven inches and weighing around 150 pounds. He bore only one physical mark to suggest that he actually was a man with a past, as he so often claimed. That mark was a bullet scar on his right leg.

At the time he signed on with the Sparks-Harrell outfit in 1895 Jack Davis had drifted around southern Idaho and northern Nevada for several years. Apparently, along the way, he had acquired something of a reputation: the first Idaho rancher who had given him a job had turned him out at gunpoint as soon as he learned the identity of the man he had hired.

Outwardly, Davis did not seem to be a cold-blooded killer. He was likable, well mannered, and kind. He was courteous to women and particularly fond of children. These attitudes may have stemmed from regrets about

[7]

his own broken family. His wife, from whom he had long been separated, had died early in 1895, leaving their seven-year-old son to be cared for by her parents.[1]

Although he probably had little education, Davis' speech was not uncouth. His greatest fault was his endless bragging, much of which had to do with his prowess as a gunman, what he called "cutting it in smoke." A modern psychiatrist would have found much to analyze in his reluctance to look you in the eye, his constant talk of shooting, his obvious lying, and his stammering.

Even though he talked a lot, his listeners knew little of the facts of his life. Presumably he was born about 1870, but the exact place remains a mystery. Various accounts of his life refer to several states as his birthplace, with Virginia being cited most frequently; West Virginia, Kentucky, and New Jersey are also mentioned.[2] His full name, Jackson Lee Davis, suggests a southern heritage.

He claimed to have spent time among the Apache Indians in Arizona, and in the mining camps of Sonora in Mexico. Later in life he claimed to have been involved in South American revolutions as a young man and to have known Cecil Rhodes in South Africa before coming to Idaho. But Davis was such a great talker that most people heavily discounted these stories. There was definite evidence concerning one part of his past, however; in 1892–93 he had worked in the Black Jack mine in the famous Silver City district of Owyhee County, Idaho. He had been a dependable, hardworking miner, but had succumbed to rumors of a diamond strike in the nearby hills and had wandered off to seek his fortune as a prospector.[3]

The diamond fields proved to be an illusion, and after a brief trip to the San Juan mining district of Colorado, Jack Davis soon came back to Idaho and Nevada. He turned to cowpunching instead of mining, and worked for a number of small ranchers on both sides of the state line. But he could not stop talking about the diamond fields. One day when Davis was working at the Stricker ranch on Rock Creek in Cassia County, Idaho, a cowboy named Bill Trotter rode in looking for him. "Where is old Diamondfield today" asked Trotter with a grin. The nickname stuck, and from that moment Jack Davis was never called anything but Diamondfield Jack by the people of Cassia County.[4]

Cassia County in the mid-1890's was a huge expanse of lush rangeland and high mountains, extending some hundred miles east and west along the southern border of Idaho. It embraced almost 5,000 square miles—about the size of Connecticut—and had a population of about 3,500. Its northern limit was the Snake River and its southern boundary was the Nevada and Utah line. Like many another western area it had prospered in an earlier era, but time and progress had since passed it by.[5] Two major transcontinental trails once had crossed it. The route of the old Oregon Trail passed along the south side of the Snake River, and thousands of pioneers had followed its dusty tracks past the settlement of Rock Creek near the present site of Twin Falls. The second great path to the Pacific was the Emigrant Trail and the Sublette Cut-off to California, which crossed from the

Snake River to the Humboldt River in Nevada by going up Raft River and Goose Creek in Cassia County.

When the Union Pacific and Central Pacific met at Promontory, Utah, in 1869 the California wagon traffic through Cassia County came to a halt, but still another trail developed which kept the area on the main line for another decade. Freight and passengers bound for Oregon now went by train to Kelton, Utah—just west of Promontory on the north side of Salt Lake—and then by stage and wagon through Cassia County to pick up the old Oregon Trail again at Rock Creek. But with the completion of the Oregon Short Line railroad across Idaho in 1883 the last link in a Pacific Northwest railroad route was finished. Unfortunately for Cassia County, the railroad route was north of the Snake River, twenty miles distant through the lava fields. So for the first time Cassia County was bypassed; no major transcontinental traffic traveled through it. As Charley Walgamott, an oldtimer in the county, explained, "While we were nearer a railroad, that great crack in the earth, Snake River Canyon, isolated us, and we became a country of whispers."

It was not just the fact that Cassia County had been relegated to the back roads of American life that put it in the mood for trouble. A full-scale range war was brewing between the well established cattlemen and the sheepmen who were coming into the area. The first cattle had been brought into southern Idaho in 1871 from Texas by A. D. Norton and M. G. Robinson, who set up ranches around Rock Creek. The following summer A. J. Harrell, a cattleman who headquartered in Visalia,

California, sent his herds from their winter ranges in the Humboldt River country of Nevada north into the Goose Creek mountains of Idaho. With James E. Bower in charge, the Harrell herd spent the summer near the Shoshone Basin.

One day from a high ridge Bower saw for the first time the broad expanse of the Snake River Valley to the north. When he rode down into the valley he met Norton, who enthusiastically showed him the possibilities of the area as a great cattle range. In those days there was very little sagebrush competing with the lush grass on the hills and ridges. In addition, the range was well watered, with the Salmon Falls River, Shoshone Creek, Big Creek, and Deep Creek all flowing year round. Bower was impressed with the land Norton had shown him, and rode back to report to his boss.

A. J. Harrell was a self-made cattle baron who had ridden over much of the West. Born in Georgia in 1830, he had joined the California gold rush in 1850. Two years later he had turned his attention to livestock, and began acquiring large tracts of grazing land. With twenty years of experience in land development, Harrell was quick to recognize the potential of this virgin Idaho range. Without delay he established the Shoe Sole ranch near Rock Creek as the newest unit of his ranch empire, and brought large numbers of cattle in from Nevada to stock it. It was a wise move; for the next ten years the Shoe Sole carried enormous herds of cattle which were profitably shipped to San Francisco. In 1882 Harrell sold just this one unit of his ranch empire to John Sparks and John Tinnin for $950,000. It was an enormous amount of money in those days, but in view of the fact that the acquisition of the Shoe Sole raised the capacity of their holdings to 175,000 head of cattle, it seemed to be a wise purchase for Sparks and Tinnin.

But the beef bonanza was ending in the West. Even though John Sparks began improving his herds with purebred Hereford, Shorthorn, and Durham stock, other forces were at work which cancelled out his efforts. Overexpansion of the industry, hard winters, drought, and overgrazing hurt the cattlemen throughout the West in the late 1880's, and the Shoe Sole was no exception. Where they had branded 38,000 calves in 1885, they branded but sixty calves in 1891. Where once the lush bunchgrass grew, now the woody sagebrush took over.

With the decline of the cattlemen in the 1880's came the rise of the sheepmen. Sheep could exist on the depleted range, although when they got through nothing else could feed after them. In 1875 the Idaho territorial legislature had recognized that the coming of sheep meant further problems; it passed an act known as the "Two Mile Limit" which prohibited sheep grazing within two miles of any possessory claim.[6] In 1887 the law was made territory-wide in application. (In a turn-of-the-century court case the Idaho Supreme Court said that Idaho would become one vast sheep range without human habitation if it were not for this law.) But, nevertheless, the number of sheep in Idaho increased by hundreds of thousands in the 1880's and early 1890's.

Although definite friction existed in Cassia County, no real trouble had developed between the cattlemen and the sheepmen. The two sides had reached a gentlemen's agreement that the sheep would stay in the eastern part of the county and the cattle in the west. The dividing line between the two ranges was the ridge that separated Goose Creek, flowing northeast into the Snake near the present town of Burley, from the waters of Deep Creek and the Salmon Falls River, which flowed northwest into the Snake in the Hagerman Valley.

Most of the people of the county lived on the sheepmen's side of the line. In this area was located the county seat of Albion, a heavily Mormon community lying in a high valley containing farms and base camps for sheep.

The cattlemen of Cassia County complained bitterly that large numbers of the sheep from this particular area were taken to the Salt Lake basin in Utah to winter so that no taxes would have to be paid on them in Idaho. This charge may have had some basis in fact, but, nevertheless, great herds of sheep still spent the winters on the high plateaus of Cassia County.

There was activity on the cattlemen's side of the line in 1895, too. John Sparks had joined forces with Andrew Harrell—the aristocratic and urbane son of the old cattle pioneer A. J. Harrell. Together, they bought out Sparks' previous partner, John Tinnin, who decided to go back to the Sand Hills of Nebraska.

John Sparks, like the senior Harrell, was an up-by-the-bootstraps cattleman and truly one of the great cattle barons of the West. Born in Mississippi in 1843, he had moved to Texas as a boy. By the time he was fourteen he was in the cattle business. He also served briefly as a Texas Ranger and an Indian scout before joining the

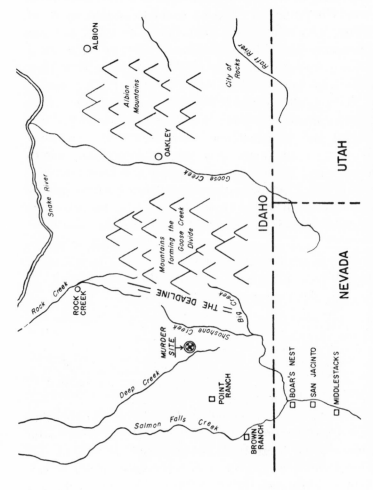

The tri-state area which formed the setting for the Diamondfield Jack case.

Union Army in the Civil War. In 1868 he arrived in Wyoming where he soon built up a sizeable cattle spread near Cheyenne. In 1880 he sold his interest to A. H. Swan, who went on to make the Swan Land & Cattle Company one of the most famous empires of the West. (Swan was the employer of the legendary Tom Horn who was hanged for a range murder in Cheyenne in 1903.) After Swan took over the Wyoming ranch, John Sparks moved to Nevada where in a few years his individual and joint holdings were even more impressive than the ones he had had before. After their merger, Sparks and Harrell owned not only the Shoe Sole near Rock Creek in Idaho, but also a string of ranches all the way south to the Humboldt River in Nevada. This massive spread consisted of 300,000 acres, supporting 40,000 head of cattle. It included the famous Alamo herd, considered the finest Hereford herd in the West. Along with a few independent ranchers such as A. D. Norton, Buck Rice, and the Jones brothers, Sparks and Harrell were the men who would have to hold the line if the sheepmen became more aggressive.

By mid-1895 the sheepmen *had* become more aggressive. Their flocks were taken across the dividing line, openly inviting the consequences. Strangers appeared at the cattle ranches, offering to work for room-and-board and no pay. The suspicious cattlemen reckoned they were detectives hired by the sheepmen. In July of that year John Sparks did what any red-blooded nineteenth-century American cattle baron would have done: he decided to fight fire with fire. He added another gunman to his payroll, in the person of Diamondfield Jack Davis.

The two other men who worked for the company in the same capacity were Billy Majors and Fred Gleason. Referred to as "outside" men because they did not perform daily ranch chores, they were paid fifty dollars a month—top money among the Sparks-Harrell hands.[7] They also got bonuses for their night riding. Their instructions came down from John Sparks through James E. Bower, the superintendent, and Joe Langford, the range foreman: "Keep the sheep back. Don't kill, but shoot to wound if necessary. Use what measures you think are best. If you do have to kill, the company will stand behind you. There is plenty of money and backing, and the company won't desert you regardless of what happens."[8]

And so Jack Davis went to work patrolling the ranges for Sparks-Harrell. It seems unlikely that he had enough of a reputation as a gunfighter to have scared the sheepmen much at first. The sobriquet "Diamondfield," which the people of the area had awarded him, pegged him as a talker; now he would have to show that he was more than that.

Within a few days after going to work for Sparks-Harrell he had his first encounter with the sheepmen. Two brothers, James and Oliver Dunn, were just across the ridge on the cattlemen's side with their sheep when Davis rode up on them. He first asked if they were Hale's men, referring to Sol Hale, a sheepman from Oakley he had been warned to watch for. The Dunn brothers replied that they were not working for Hale.

Davis seemed satisfied. "It's a good thing," he told them, "because there would have been fighting if you had been Hale's men." During this encounter Davis explained that he had been hired by Sparks and Bower to protect the range, and that he was on "fighting wages." In parting he told the Dunns, "If the sheep come any farther you'll be facing the muzzle of a Winchester."

Late in the summer Davis had a similar run-in with William Craner, a herder who had taken a band of Oliver Dunn's sheep up against the line. He told Craner that he was going to kill someone that summer or be killed himself. "I'll shoe my horse with rawhide," bragged Diamondfield Jack, "and Jesus Christ himself couldn't track me. I Apachied it once, and I still know how." Before he left Craner he repeated his threat, specifically saying that he would kill Sol Hale and Bill Tolman, another sheepman from the Oakley district. A pattern was now beginning to develop in the intimidation of the sheepmen: Diamondfield Jack was always currently gunning for a sheepman who, conveniently, was somewhere else at the moment.

Still later that year Davis and Billy Majors were riding together when they ran across Jesse Wilson, who was also herding for Oliver Dunn, on the cattlemen's side of the ridge. Majors did most of the talking on this occasion, but Davis told Wilson that there were three men hired to keep the sheep out and they could easily get twenty-five men if they needed them.

The next encounter was with a herder named Jabez Durfee. On this occasion Davis made it clear to him that he could not bring his sheep across the line. "I'll kill the next sheepherder who crosses that ridge," avowed Davis. He singled out two sheepmen as special enemies, saying that he wanted Bill Tolman to cross over so that he could use him for a target, and that he wanted Jesse Wilson to cross the ridge and discover the trouble he would get into on the cattlemen's side.

By the time Davis met William Orr on the range a bit later, tempers had begun to fray. Davis was in the process of threatening Orr if he brought his sheep over, when a herder in Orr's camp suddenly moved. Diamondfield Jack whipped out his gun and covered the man. The herders did not retaliate, however, and when calm returned to the conversation Davis explained in the peculiar chivalry of the cowman that he was holding the range for the honor of it, not for the money involved. He referred to the dividing ridge as the "deadline," across which Orr was not to take his sheep.

Up to this point the show-downs had been verbal rather than physical. But there were now signs that the harassment by Diamondfield Jack was beginning to make the sheepmen jumpy. Both sides had long since been packing guns, not just because there were cougar, bear, and coyotes nearby. J. H. Foxley, a cattleman from the west end of the county, came across a group of sheepmen on the range. When he rode up with a friendly "Hello" he found himself facing drawn guns. One of the sheepmen, E. R. Dayley, explained, "We thought you were Diamondfield." When they saw that he was not their special enemy, the sheepmen put away their guns and became as friendly as the strained situation permitted.

Even though range war was now imminent, there was a strange kind of relationship existing through the latter part of 1895—a kind of man-in-the-open camaraderie. Even Jack Davis in threatening the sheepherders was apt to break off the argument long enough to have a cup of coffee or a meal with his adversaries. And, when the tensions boiled over in November into the first real bloodshed, it all seemed more like a comic opera than a classic showdown of the old West.

Bill Tolman, whom Davis had never met, finally accepted the word-of-mouth invitation to cross the ridge. On November 15 he rode up to a Sparks-Harrell line shack in the Shoshone Basin and confronted Diamondfield Jack with a rifle. After a long argument Jack saw his chance, pulled his .45, and shot Tolman through the shoulder. The sheepman, in great pain, lost his bravado and wanted help. Davis examined the wound, and made his victim as comfortable as possible. He then shouted to a group of sheepmen on a nearby hill to come over and get Tolman. But the sheepmen were reluctant to get any closer to Diamondfield Jack. After yelling in vain, Davis finally helped Tolman down the hill to the sheep camp where he left him to be picked up by his friends. The sight of the wounded sheepman being carried back to Oakley that day was enough to discourage other herders bound for the area, and for the next few weeks the sheepmen were considerably less aggressive than before.

Diamondfield Jack was no fool. He knew he was in trouble. After openly threatening to kill Tolman, he had put himself in jeopardy by actually wounding the man. He would have a hard time convincing a jury of sheepmen that he had shot in self-defense, and a much harder time, if Tolman should die, of convincing a lynch mob. Discreetly he headed south into Nevada to lie low until things calmed down. On the way he collected his pay and terminated his brief relationship with Sparks-Harrell. He headed for Wells, Nevada— mecca for all saddle-sore cowboys on the Sparks-Harrell circuit. In the warmth of Fischer's saloon there, and in the carnal comforts of Alice Wood's palace of pleasure, he soon forgot the unpleasantness of the past few months. Without realizing it, he was enjoying his last fling at freedom before a maze of circumstance closed in around him.

NOTES

[1] The story of the rancher running Diamondfield Jack off his place is told in Charles S. Walgamott, *Six Decades Back*. The facts concerning Davis' marriage are from his long deposition to the pardon board in 1901.

[2] The birthplaces are mentioned in histories and obituaries. Lynchburg, Virginia, is cited most frequently, but the Virginia Bureau of Vital Records is unable to find a birth certificate for him in the records for 1868–1873.

[3] In depositions Davis mentioned the time he spent among Apache Indians, in Mexican mining camps, and in Central America. His claim to experience in South American revolutions appears in a letter cited in John F. MacLane, *A Sagebrush Lawyer*. The only early reference to these military experiences was in an article on Davis in *Successful American* for August, 1906. His Idaho mining experience was verified in a letter from the mine foreman to the pardon board. The "diamond excitement" is described in Davis' deposition to the pardon board, and is confirmed in the *Caldwell* [Idaho] *Tribune* for December of 1892.

[4] The story of the nickname is told in Walgamott. Davis' depositions generally confirm it, particularly with regard to Bill Trotter originating the name.

⁵The early history of Cassia County is explained in Walgamott.

⁶The "Two Mile Limit" is explained in MacLane, who cites *Sweet* v. *Ballentine,* 69 Pacific 995.

⁷The arrangements under which the "outside" men were employed were described in a registered letter from K. I. Perky to James Hawley, December 2, 1897. Perky obtained the information from William Majors, one of the "outside" men. The letter is preserved in the Hawley collection of the Idaho Historical Society. The various encounters with sheepmen are related in the trial testimony.

⁸Perky's letter to Hawley.

Cattle baron John Sparks (second from left) shares chuck wagon fare with ranch hands about 1900. Diamondfield Jack was Sparks' troubleshooter. (Courtesy of Nevada Historical Society)

2

The Affair on Deep Creek

FOR THE next few weeks the recollection of Bill Tolman's experience with Diamondfield Jack kept the sheepmen off the cattle ranges. But before long they realized that Jack Davis did not seem to be around any more. Soon they were pushing across the line again, and by the end of January, 1896, herds had been taken almost to the Salmon Falls River near the western edge of the county. The range was crawling with sheep and with armed sheepherders.

Cautiously, Jack Davis came out of hiding. He crossed over from the Humboldt into the Salmon Falls valley and began going down the river, stopping at the various Sparks-Harrell ranches along the way—the HD, the Vineyard, the Middlestacks, the San Jacinto, the Boar's Nest. He thought about riding on north to Albion and giving himself up for the Tolman shooting, but the prospect of facing the irate sheepmen was too much. The last of January found him at the Middle-

stacks ranch on the Salmon Falls River on the Nevada
—and safe—side of the line.

Fred Gleason was there, too. Gleason was an impet-
uous young local cowhand who was well thought of
around the area, although he was one of the "outside"
men hired by Sparks-Harrell to intimidate the sheepherders. At the Middlestacks Davis and Gleason lounged
around for a couple of days, engaging in two favorite
activities of cowhands: swapping stories and practicing
their shooting. Occasionally a coyote came close enough
to provide a shot for a Winchester, but most of the time
the men used their six-shooters on cans and boxes.
Gleason used a .44, but Davis was forced to give up
shooting his .45 when he ran out of shells—unless he
wanted to use .44 ammunition. Also at the ranch were
Harve Tranmer and Frank Smith. Tranmer worked out
of the Brown ranch in Idaho, and Smith was a cowboy
who hung around the Sparks-Harrell ranches even
though he had been fired a couple of months earlier.

Diamondfield Jack was wearing a canvas hunting
jacket when he came to the Middlestacks. Before leaving the ranch he traded it to Frank Smith for a darker
and heavier coat, saying that the canvas one was "too
light." Smith and Tranmer were not sure whether Jack
meant it was too light in weight for the winter days
ahead, or too light in color for the kind of night riding
Davis had previously been doing. At any rate, Davis
and Gleason left the Middlestacks the next day and
headed downriver for the Brown ranch on the Idaho
side of the state line. Davis was riding a buckskin horse,
and Gleason a bay called Sandow. Both men were

heavily armed, and somewhere along the way they had acquired a number of sticks of dynamite. They said they were going out to look for two horses—Idaho, who was out on the range somewhere, and Beady, who had been at another ranch but belonged back at the Middlestacks.

On February 1, 1896, Harve Tranmer of the Brown ranch brought Beady back to that ranch and turned him over to Davis and Gleason, who had arrived earlier. Tranmer explained that the horse was somewhat lame as a result of hard riding at the hands of a cowboy from the Jones ranch. Unknown to Diamondfield Jack, this hard-riding cowboy—Jeff Gray—was to play a dramatic role in his life. The following day Gleason and Davis rode east from the Brown ranch in midafternoon, Gleason on Beady, a favorite of his, and Davis on the buckskin. Nobody knows exactly what they were up to that day, but they provoked—either by accident or design—another shooting skirmish of the range war.[1]

About nine o'clock that night near Point ranch, seven or eight miles northeast of the Brown ranch and well into the state of Idaho, Davis and Gleason came upon a sheep camp in the darkness. Although there was no way of Diamondfield Jack's knowing, it was a camp belonging to his earlier adversary, Oliver Dunn, the sheepman. The tinkling bell of a hobbled horse was the first warning of the sheep camp's presence. As Jack Davis' finger closed around the trigger of his Winchester his horse spooked and the gun fired. Fred Gleason reined his horse around quickly and headed for safety. Inside the sheep camp the herders, Joseph Wilson and his brother Loren, jumped into action. They grabbed rifles, and began firing into the darkness. Davis was no coward. He kept the buckskin moving in a circle around the camp while he continued firing toward the herders. Finally, after each side had fired about a dozen shots, Diamondfield Jack broke off the action and rode away. He soon overtook Gleason, and the two men returned to the Brown ranch around ten o'clock that night.

The brief fight produced only one casualty: a horse was killed in the sheep camp. The skirmish might have been completely overlooked in the light of later events, were it not for the fact that Davis—and Gleason, too— was soon bragging about a "shooting scrape" with sheepherders. It may have been this affair to which they referred, or it may have been another affair far graver.

On the third of February Davis and Gleason stayed around the Brown ranch. It snowed some during the day, so when they decided to shoe Beady they had to work in the barn. Gleason talked freely with Harve Tranmer; he told him that while Tranmer had been up north to get Beady a local cattleman named Billy Walker had stopped at the ranch, and that Gleason had introduced Diamondfield Jack to him as Miller—rather than let it be known that Jack was back on the range. He also told Tranmer about the incident at the sheep camp the night before.

On the morning of the fourth they rode out from the Brown ranch about sunup, Gleason again on the bay horse, Beady, and Diamondfield Jack on the buckskin. They told Harve Tranmer they were going back up the river to the Middlestacks, and asked about a ford two miles above. This seemed a bit odd to Tranmer since there was a bridge spanning the river right where they were—at the Brown ranch. Also, both the Brown ranch and the Middlestacks were on the same side—the west side—of the river. But the ranch foreman was used to the wandering ways of cowboys and drifters, so he gave it little thought as he watched the two men ride up the narrow canyon toward the Nevada line. A couple of days later, though, when he found dynamite hidden away in the bunkhouse where Davis and Gleason had been sleeping, Harve Tranmer again began to wonder about the two "outside" men.

On the same morning that Davis and Gleason left the Brown ranch, some fifteen miles to the northeast another link in a chain of fateful circumstances was being fashioned. Two sheepherders, John Wilson and Daniel Cummings, had set up their camp on a rolling hillside on Deep Creek, well over into the forbidden cattle range. They were busy preparing breakfast when Davis Hunter, another herder whose sheep were camped even farther to the west, came by their camp. He dropped off a load of firewood from his two-wheeled cart before continuing on to Oakley, a day's ride to the east. Everything was normal about the camp. The two sheepdogs were tied to the wheels of the wagon, the sheep were close by, and Wilson and Cummings were in good spirits when Hunter left a quarter of an hour later.

On February 16, twelve days later, another herder working nearby, Edgar Severe, noticed some scattered bands of sheep. When he went to investigate he encountered a grisly scene. Wilson and Cummings were both in the wagon. They had been shot to death. Severe rode back to his own camp northwest of the Wilson-Cummings camp and dispatched a young rider named Noel Carlson to notify the authorities at Oakley, some thirty miles to the east. The word was then relayed to the sheriff at Albion, another twenty miles northeast, by Andrew Day on the seventeenth.

While waiting for the sheriff and coroner to arrive, the sheepmen near Deep Creek generally stayed away from the camp of the murdered men. However, Davis Hunter entered the camp on the seventeenth to release the dogs which were still tied to the wagon wheels. They were so thin and emaciated that they could hardly bark or growl, but with food, water, and attention in the other camp, they soon recovered.

On February 18, 1896, the sheriff's party finally reached the murder scene after a ride of well over fifty miles on horseback and by cart. Harvey Perkins was a sheepman, as well as being sheriff of Cassia County. He and the county coroner, Dr. R. T. Story, made an examination of the camp and of the bodies, but they were careless about handling the evidence and consequently some of the best opportunities to determine what had actually happened were lost. Furthermore, a number of sheepmen came with the sheriff and coroner, and their tramping around the camp and handling of the evidence made things even worse.

The sheep wagon was typical of those used then and now on western ranges. It had a wooden body with projecting sideboards which ran the length of the wagon. A semicircular canvas canopy went over the top from one sideboard to the other. The bunk was across the back end. Wilson's body lay diagonally across the bunk, covered with an overcoat. Cummings' body was crumpled at the foot of the bunk.[2]

Dr. Story performed an autopsy on each man on the ground nearby. He found Wilson's body "badly decomposed, purple in color, and emitting an offensive odor." Cummings' body was only partially decomposed. The coroner judged that Wilson had lived only a few hours after being shot, while Cummings might have lived as long as a day and a half. Each man had been shot once. Wilson had a gaping wound in his chin. Powdermarks on his hand and face indicated that he had been shot at close range. The bullet had gone through the body and lodged in his clothing. Cummings had been shot through the abdomen.

There were plenty of clues. There was blood on the ground close to the wagon tongue, and a bullet hole through the tongue itself, beneath which a slug was found in a coal oil can. Another bullet hole went through the right hand side of the wagon box. A bloody handprint was found on the canvas curtains at the front of the wagon. Under Cummings was a piece of paper on which the dying man had scrawled, "If I die, bury me. Take care of my sisters." Another significant clue was a corncob pipe found between the front wheels of the wagon, a pipe which had been smoked only a few times. The sheriff and coroner found no tobacco or other evidence of smoking in the camp; the other sheepherders who were present assured the officials that the two young Mormon men had not been smokers.

Three empty .44 cartridges were found strung out in a line behind the wagon. The slugs found in the wagon and in the can matched them. There was a .45–70 caliber rifle in the wagon, but it had not been fired since its last cleaning. Two unfired shells for this gun were discovered, one in Cummings' pocket and one on the bunk under his body.

In attempting to reconstruct the crime the sheriff guessed from the emaciated condition of the dogs, and from some dried but unbaked dough in the campstove oven near the front of the wagon, that the men must have been killed shortly after Davis Hunter had seen them on the fourth of February. Dr. Story confirmed this theory by his estimate of the length of time the men had been dead. So the sheriff, as he rounded up the evidence and the bystanders and herded them all back to Albion, must have realized that the time lag had put him at a definite disadvantage. The murderer could be out of the county, the state, or even the country by now.

In the beginning, the clues could have provided some good leads, but since neither the sheriff nor the coroner firmly took charge of the evidence, some of it was actually lost. For example, both the sheriff and the coroner lost track of the note Cummings had written. In addition, the corncob pipe was picked up by a sheepman named McMurray who kept it for awhile before turning it over to another sheepman named Gray. The clothing of the dead men had similar treatment. T. M. Cummings, uncle of the dead sheepherder, took possession of it initially. Later he gave it to William Quinn, the deputy sheriff, who gave it to W. E. Pierson, the

justice-of-the-peace, who eventually passed it on to the
clerk of the district court. The cartridges received even
worse handling, as we shall see shortly.

But evidence may not have been the most important
thing to the aroused sheepmen back in Albion. When
word of the tragedy first reached the eastern part of the
county, reaction was swift and predictable. The cattlemen were blamed for the killing. Specifically, the sheepmen pointed the finger of guilt at their particular enemy,
Diamondfield Jack Davis. Public opinion was so aroused
that rumors of an armed invasion of the cattle country
were soon heard throughout the county.

Diamondfield Jack's movements since leaving the
Brown ranch could be traced fairly well. On the first day
he had acted innocent enough, but later he began to be-
have more like a guilty man. Foreman Harve Tranmer
had watched Davis and Gleason leave the Brown ranch
headed toward Nevada about sun-up on the fourth, the
day of the murder. The next time the men were seen
was about one o'clock in the afternoon of the same day.
This was when C. D. Edwards, Sparks-Harrell foreman
at the Boar's Nest, the first ranch on the Nevada side,
returned to the ranch to find Davis and Gleason finishing their dinner there. He saw their horses, Beady and
the buckskin, who did not look as if they had been ridden very hard. That afternoon Davis and Gleason rode
deeper south in Nevada to the Middlestacks ranch with
four horses. Gleason was on the bay horse, Sandow,
and leading Beady; Davis was riding a sorrel and leading his buckskin. Henry Harris, the Negro foreman, met
them at the Middlestacks about mid-afternoon. He, too,

did not think the horses looked as if they had been ridden hard.

That evening Diamondfield Jack traded the dark coat back to Frank Smith and got his own hunting jacket in return. After spending the night at the Middlestacks, Davis and Gleason rode still further south in Nevada the next morning, February 5, to the Vineyard ranch, twelve miles away. On the following day they rode on to the HD ranch where they encountered James E. Bower, the superintendent for Sparks-Harrell, who had ridden down across the state line from the Shoe Sole ranch in Idaho. The three men rode on to the Nevada hamlet of Wells and stayed that night at the Hardesty House, a hotel run by C. B. Moore. It is significant that in this chance encounter with James Bower, Diamondfield Jack sensed nothing unusual in the superintendent's demeanor.

Bower was looking for owner John Sparks who was starting east with a shipment of cattle, so he headed for Reno to intercept him there. Davis and Gleason found themselves once again without responsibilities or supervision in the relaxing atmosphere of their favorite town. Both of them immediately began the cowboy's rest cure: women and drink. When their tongues were well loosened by liquor they began talking indiscreetly about a shooting up in Idaho.

After about a week Davis wearied of town, so he began visiting some of his old Nevada haunts. He dropped into the Lamoille Valley at the foot of the Ruby Range, some thirty-five miles southwest of Wells. Here he stopped at the Hayward ranch for a few days.

Mrs. Emily Hayward, for whom Jack Davis had worked briefly the previous summer, found him on this occasion rather apprehensive and fearful of the law. He told her something of his work for the cattle company but, true to form, he embellished it considerably. He told her that he had been making $150 a month, and that the Sparks-Harrell company had promised to stand behind him if he got into trouble. He confessed that he had gotten involved in a shooting scrape, and that he had probably killed a man. An interested listener to these conversations was Randolph Streeter, Mrs. Hayward's eighteen-year-old son; he got the impression that Davis had shot two men in Idaho.

Another of Diamondfield Jack's old friends in the Lamoille Valley was J. B. Gheen, who ran a general store and served as justice of the peace. One night, heavily armed, Jack paid a visit to his store. In the presence of some strangers Davis boasted that he had "shot up" two sheepherders in Idaho. It was a drunken boast, but by now word of the killing of Wilson and Cummings had reached even this isolated community and it was easy for people to conclude that Diamondfield Jack was admitting the crime on Deep Creek. Davis did not help things by announcing to all present that he was deliberately dodging Sheriff Mateer of Elko County.

As yet, the fundamental question of the whole affair had not even arisen. Was Diamondfield Jack referring to the murder of Wilson and Cummings on Deep Creek or was he simply bragging about his nighttime exchange of shots with the herders at the Dunn camp? The question had not been raised because the Dunn camp affair was not a matter of common knowledge, while the killing of the two sheepherders was. Thus, people assumed that when he spoke of a shooting in Idaho he was referring to the Deep Creek affair, and the impression grew that Diamondfield Jack was the murderer. After his visit to the Lamoille Valley, people who were once his friends there were ready to think the worst of him. At Deeth, midway between Wells and Lamoille, Diamondfield Jack made another incriminating statement that could easily be interpreted as an admission of guilt in the Deep Creek affair. When George Porter, a merchant who was selling him a new Stetson, commented on how much money Jack was carrying, Davis replied, "I'm getting forty dollars a month for shooting sheepherders." This statement about the size of his pay was probably truer than some of the things he bragged about to his old friends in the Lamoille Valley, but there was still the same characteristic half-truth and innuendo out of which his listeners could draw whatever conclusion they chose.

Late in February, 1896, Diamondfield Jack paid his last visit to a Sparks-Harrell ranch. He drifted into the Middlestacks where he spent a few days trying to find out how things looked for him. He told cowboy Frank Smith about the nighttime incident at the Dunn sheep camp, and how Gleason had fled. He was worried about Gleason who had been getting drunk at Wells and talking about killing sheepherders on Deep Creek. As a result, public opinion in the Nevada town was hostile to Gleason and Davis. Jack was in trouble again. This time he thought he had better put more than a state line between himself and the irate Idaho sheepmen of Albion. He asked Smith how much money a man needed to leave the country, and the cowboy ventured that at least a couple of hundred dollars was necessary. Apparently Diamondfield Jack either had the money or managed to get it, because a few days later he started south on horseback, following the back roads all the way. Gleason, too, headed for parts unknown.

Meanwhile, things were coming to a boil at Albion. The sheepmen were certain that Diamondfield Jack was the murderer, and they wanted him brought to trial. A criminal complaint was sworn against Davis and Gleason on March 20, 1896, legally charging them with the double murder. Through their local and state associations the sheepmen raised several rewards. A thousand dollars was offered specifically for Davis on the charge of the attempted murder of Bill Tolman, growing out of the altercation in the Shoshone Basin in November when Diamondfield Jack shot the sheepman in the shoulder. Half of the reward was furnished by the state of Idaho and half by the Idaho Wool Growers Association. An additional $3,600 was offered for the capture of the murderer of Cummings and Wilson— $1,000 each from the state and the Cassia County Wool Growers, $800 from the county commissioners, $500 from the Idaho Wool Growers, and $300 from private individuals.

There was also a remarkable amount of money available to hire detectives and attorneys. Persistent rumor had it that some of this money came from the coffers of the Mormon Church in Salt Lake City, since the two murdered sheepherders had been Mormons.[3] It began to look as though far more than just a range killing incident was involved. With this money the sheepmen moved quickly and effectively. Out of their substantial treasury they hired a bright young Boise attorney by the name of William E. Borah.

Borah was well known around the state, but by no means had he yet become the "Lion of Idaho" in national politics. Born in Illinois in 1865, Borah had gone to Kansas in the 1880's. After a brief career as a country school teacher, he had entered the University of Kansas in 1885. When poor health ended his college work a year later, he spent some time convalescing in the home of his sister, who was married to a lawyer in western Kansas. To spend the long hours profitably, he read a great number of books—including some law books belonging to his brother-in-law. Along with a return to good health, the year 1887 saw Borah passing a fairly simple bar examination and launching his career as a lawyer. But things were slow for an ambitious young man—even a lawyer—in western Kansas in those days. Seeking greater opportunity, Borah headed west in 1890 with a vague determination to locate in the Pacific Northwest.

On the train he met a gambler from Nampa, Idaho—the mainline junction point for the Boise branch of the railroad. The gambler persuaded him that Boise would offer good possibilities for a young lawyer. He even offered to throw some business his way to help him get started. With this inducement, William E. Borah arrived in Boise with $15.75 in his pocket.

His law practice began inauspiciously. His first case, which he got through the help of the gambler from Nampa, was the defense of a Chinese man accused of murder. Borah's case was weak, but his luck and determination were sizable. He won, and his career in Idaho was underway. Success came quickly; within a few years he had a large practice, involving now the respectable element of town rather than the sporting element. He also became influential in state Republican politics. He was pegged as a "comer" in both the law and politics. The Diamondfield Jack case was Borah's first big break, and he was anxious—perhaps too much so—to make a reputation with it.

After reviewing the facts Borah decided that Diamondfield Jack was indeed the key to the case. In the garb of a cowboy the young attorney rode the circuit of Sparks-Harrell ranches talking to the men who had worked with Davis, and trying to find out what had happened on the fourth of February. When he had to identify himself, he posed as a ranch buyer. On this ride Borah gathered some useful information, but he failed to turn up any direct knowledge of the whereabouts of Diamondfield Jack or Fred Gleason.[4]

With $4,600 in rewards riding on Davis' head it was natural that overzealous lawmen around the West would soon be reporting that they had captured the man that Cassia County wanted. In midsummer of 1896 a legal requisition was sent to Shawnee, Oklahoma, for a cowboy arrested there who fit Davis' description quite closely. He was of the same size and coloring, he had a bullet scar on the leg, and he stuttered badly when he was drunk. However, he was not Diamondfield Jack. Another false lead came from Santa Rosa, California. The man who was jailed there as Jack Davis was photographed and the picture sent to the Cassia County authorities. A number of sheepmen positively identified the picture as that of Diamondfield Jack. But when the authorities went to Santa Rosa to get this man they discovered that he, too, was the wrong one. So Diamondfield Jack remained at large.

During his sojourn at the Sparks-Harrell ranches Borah had found that some of the company's men seemed to dislike Gleason and Davis intensely while others counted them as real friends. This situation seemed to offer good possibilities for a skillful lawyer. By playing one group against the other, Borah found Gleason and eventually got a lead on where Davis was hiding. It turned out to be an unlikely spot.

Frank Smith, the cowboy whom John Sparks had fired in November of 1895, saw a chance to share in the $4,600 reward and also to get back at the cattle company by capitalizing on his jealousy of the "outside" men. He reported to Borah that Doc Goodin, a Sparks-Harrell man, was getting letters from Gleason and Davis. When it was necessary to get possession of some of the letters to discover where they came from, Smith seems to have taken the simplest expedient: he rifled Goodin's pants pockets. One letter showed that Gleason was holed up in Deer Lodge, Montana. Apparently through Smith's conversations with Goodin, Borah also learned that

Davis was even farther away—in the territorial prison in Yuma, Arizona![5]

A quick exchange of correspondence with the prison warden in February, 1897, confirmed the fact that Diamondfield Jack Davis was indeed a prisoner at the famous—or infamous—penitentiary. It had happened this way. Shortly after arriving in Arizona in April of 1896 Davis had gotten into a fracas in the town of Congress. It started when he shot a dog which had been harassing his horse. A policeman was summoned by the boy who owned the dog. Davis held up the policeman, took his pistol, and disarmed another officer who sought to help the first one. Finally a local citizen came to the rescue of the officers and knocked Davis down with a shotgun blast. For this behavior, officially designated as "Aggravated Battery," Diamondfield Jack earned himself a year in prison. He entered under the name of Frank Woodson because, as he explained it later, someone kept shouting the name "Woodson" during the melee at Congress.

Conditions in the territorial prison at Yuma were notoriously bad, and Davis was hardly an ideal prisoner. He managed to escape once, but was recaptured on the streets of Yuma after three and a half hours of freedom. A stretch in solitary confinement failed to dampen his aggressiveness, however, and he was soon back in solitary for fighting with another inmate. Thus he could not have been too unhappy when Oliver P. Anderson, the newly-elected Cassia County sheriff, arrived in March of 1897 to take him back to Idaho. Furthermore, the Arizona authorities must have been glad to get rid of him.[6]

With Sheriff Anderson were two sheepmen, J. J. Gray and E. R. Dayley. Dayley had been deputized for the trip. He was hardly acting out of a pure sense of civic duty, since the sheep raisers' association was paying his expenses on the trip. Also, he had contributed part of the reward money himself. The three men put handcuffs and leg irons on Diamondfield Jack for the long railroad journey back to Idaho. In the day coach going through Nevada (not far from the point where another man named Jack Davis, no relation, had pulled the first train robbery in the West some twenty-five years earlier) Davis received a telegram from John Sparks, assuring support from the cattle company. This seemed to bolster his courage and to lessen his hostility; Davis began talking to Dayley, assuring the deputy that he had no firsthand knowledge of the crime.

While Davis was being returned to Idaho, John Sparks was keeping his word to stand behind his gunmen—regardless of what happened. Since the battles would now be fought in the courts instead of on the range, Sparks hired a notoriously bad shot but an exceptionally good lawyer, James H. Hawley of Boise.

Hawley was a prototype of the circuit-riding "sagebrush lawyer," and perhaps the greatest criminal lawyer in the entire West. Born in Iowa in 1847, he first came to Idaho as a youth of fifteen when the area was still part of Washington Territory. From 1863 until 1865 he mined gold in the Boise Basin, accumulating enough money to finance two years of college education in San Francisco. After an adventurous post-graduation trip to the Orient, Hawley returned to the mining camps of the new Idaho Territory in 1869. The following year he began his forty-year career of public service to the territory and the state, a career which made him one of the best known and best liked men in Idaho. In rapid succession he was elected to the lower house of the legislature, admitted to the territorial bar, elected to the upper house of the legislature, was appointed District Attorney for central Idaho, and was named United States Attorney for the territory. In this latter capacity Hawley was called upon to prosecute the Latter Day Saints for polygamy, but he remained personally tolerant toward the Mormons even though one wing of the Democratic party in Idaho was making political hay from anti-Mormonism. Hawley led the other wing of the party; he was a conservative who believed in a minimum of restriction on personal freedom.

As a criminal lawyer James Hawley was an Idaho legend. His biographer, John MacLane, has said that during Hawley's career he was involved in more murder cases as prosecutor or defense attorney than any other American lawyer in history, with the total running over three hundred. Several years earlier he had achieved a great legal triumph in defending a number of union miners accused of murder and mayhem in the Coeur d'Alene mining riots of 1892. Most of these men were acquitted, and only a few received sentences—and these were light. Hawley was at the height of his power and prestige in 1897; he was the logical choice to defend Jack Davis before an Idaho jury.[7]

Gleason was returned from Montana and indicted along with Davis. The trial of each man was set for the

April, 1897, term of district court with Judge C. O. Stockslager presiding. Officially the prosecution would be headed by John C. Rogers, the bearded Cassia County prosecutor. But in Idaho special prosecutors were often used in addition to the regular local staff, and Borah's name was entered as a special prosecutor for the state. Still another special prosecutor, O. W. Powers, was brought in from Salt Lake City.

Orlando Woodworth Powers was a lawyer of considerable reputation, too. Born in New York in 1851, he had graduated in law from the University of Michigan in 1871. In 1885 he was appointed by President Cleveland to the Supreme Court of the Territory of Utah. Like Hawley, he was active in the Democratic party organization in his state. He had been chairman of the Gentile party of Utah in its campaign against the Mormons in 1888, so it is unlikely that he was sent out from Salt Lake City by "Mormon money," but he was generally considered to be the leading criminal lawyer of Utah, so his presence on the prosecution staff strengthened it considerably.

Hawley had two colleagues in his defense of Diamondfield Jack. One was Will Puckett, his young law partner from Boise, who was to prove highly valuable and resourceful in the months to come. The other was Kirtland I. Perky, onetime law partner of William Jennings Bryan in Nebraska, now a Cassia County attorney whose direct knowledge of the local situation made him indispensable to Hawley.

The trial of Jack Davis, alias Diamondfield Jack, for the murder of John C. Wilson began April 5, 1897, with the formal arraignment of the defendant in the old courthouse at Albion, a two-story frame building which had been built as a hotel some years earlier. It was not a widely-heralded trial which brought newsmen from any distance. On the contrary, it was a local grudge fight, intensified by the presence of high-powered out-of-town lawyers paid for by wealthy sheep raisers' associations and by even wealthier cattle barons. It promised to bring back briefly to Cassia County some of the excitement and color it had known in the days of the Oregon Trail and the California Trail. But before the struggle was over it would prove to be far more than prosecution versus defense, or even cattlemen against sheepmen. It would pit Mormon against Gentile, and Republican against Democrat, creating one of the strangest legal dramas in the history of the West.

NOTES

[1]Davis' actions early in February, 1896, are reconstructed from various testimony at his trial.

[2]The scene of the murder was described by witnesses during the trial.

[3]The reward money was itemized on notices sent to law enforcement officials. Concerning the rumors of "Mormon money" behind the prosecution, the historian of the Church of Jesus Christ of Latter Day Saints can find no reference to cattle-sheep trouble or to any money spent in this connection in the records of the Cassia County stake.

[4]Borah's visits to the Sparks-Harrell ranches are described in C. P. Connolly, "Presidential Possibilities: Borah of Idaho," *Collier's,* July 31, 1915. Connolly was a close personal friend and confidant of Borah.

[5]The process by which the authorities located Gleason and Davis is reconstructed from testimony and depositions.

[6]The circumstances surrounding Davis' imprisonment at Yuma are from his own explanations in various depositions.

[7]For an assessment of James Hawley as an attorney see John Mac-Lane, *A Sagebrush Lawyer;* Albert L. Lewis, "Sagebrush Rhetoric: The Oratory of James H. Hawley," unpublished Ph.D. dissertation, University of Oregon, 1967; David H. Grover, *Debaters and Dynamiters: The Story of the Haywood Trial.* E. F. Richardson, who teamed with Clarence Darrow in opposing Hawley and Borah in the Haywood trial in 1907, called his adversaries "the two greatest lawyers in the state of Idaho and I am willing to concede perhaps the two greatest lawyers in all of the west." Grover, p. 201.

3

The State vs. Jack Davis

ON April 8, 1897, Cassia County prosecutor John C. Rogers made his opening remarks to the jury. He might have sensed that he was something of a junior partner to the high-powered special prosecutors from Boise and Salt Lake—even though he was actually the oldest of the three attorneys for the state—but he gave no indication that he had surrendered his responsibility as district attorney of the county.

Rogers had been born in Tennessee in 1843, but spent most of his boyhood in Missouri. After attending William Jewell College he had enlisted in the 6th Missouri Cavalry of the Union Army during the Civil War. Like Diamonfield Jack, whom he was now prosecuting, John Rogers carried a bullet in his leg, but his was a souvenir of the war. During the tense days of reconstruction in Missouri, Rogers had studied law and passed the bar examination. His health was broken, however, and he was forced to travel widely seeking a favorable climate in which to practice. He had settled in

Denver for three years, then moved on to Virginia City and Glendale, Montana. During his stay in Montana he had become active in Democratic politics and was elected to the state legislature. When his health failed again he spent a year recuperating in the mountains of Nevada and California. He had come to Cassia County in 1888, and the dry brisk air had apparently agreed with him for he stayed on and prospered in Albion— first as an attorney and more recently as county prosecutor.

Rogers had been talking to a jury whom he had every reason to trust. It had taken only a day and a half to examine the panel and to select the jurors acceptable to both sides. But the defense had no real chance of getting jurors favorably disposed toward Diamondfield Jack, so all that Hawley and Perky could hope for was a group of men who would take their responsibility seriously.

Every one of the jurors was from the sheepmen's side of Goose Creek divide, the "deadline" of the range war. H. R. Cahoon, foreman of the jury, was from the Raft River country in the easternmost part of the county, as were George T. Moore, M. F. Durfee, J. W. Miller, B. O. Barker, Thomas Bates, Robert Wake, and S. H. Barker. Four others were from the Albion area: John Clark, Stephen Mahoney, E. H. Schmidt, and George W. Gray. All of the jurors were farmers, excepting Miller, who was a miner.

The prosecution opened its case on April 8 by calling as its first witness Harvey L. Perkins, who had been the sheriff at the time the crime was discovered. He described how he had been summoned to Deep Creek to investigate the shooting, and what had been found in the camp—the shells, the note, the corncob pipe, and other clues.[1] He identified two slugs introduced in evidence as those taken from the bodies of Wilson and Cummings. He admitted that he had seen the note written by Cummings but that he did not know what had happened to it since then. (Later the note was introduced in evidence, but no one was able to swear that it was the same note found at the scene.) On cross-examination Perkins described the vicinity of the killing as rough country, rocky and cut up by canyons. He also admitted that he was a sheepman, and, although not a member of the association, he had helped get the reward together for the capture of Diamondfield Jack. He concluded his testimony by venturing an opinion that the gun that killed Wilson had been fired no more than three feet from him—perhaps closer.

Dr. R. T. Story, the coroner, testified next and confirmed much of what the sheiff had said about the scene of the crime. He said that there had been "four or five" empty cartridges there, but admitted that all but one of these cartridges had been lost during the year that he had had custody of them. The shells had been on display in a cabinet in his office, and he thought that perhaps his small daughter had been playing with them. But he identified the one shell remaining, a .44, as one picked up at the scene of the crime.

Edgar Severe, the sheepman, then described the circumstances of finding the bodies, sending word to the sheriff, and releasing the dogs. Several other men who had been in the original party to visit the scene explained how they had come to have some of the evidence in their possession at various times. Up to this point the prosecution was showing primarily that a crime had been committed, and that it was done at the time and place alleged in the indictment.

Now began the testimony designed to link up Diamondfield Jack with the killing. J. H. Foxley of Sparks-Harrell explained that he had turned over the company's purebred herd in Shoshone Basin to Jack Davis in the summer of 1895. He also recounted his experiences with the sheepmen who pulled guns on him, thinking he was Davis. Then the various sheepherders whom Davis had threatened that summer and fall told their stories. James and Oliver Dunn, William Orr, Jesse Wilson, William Craner, and Jabez Durfee all described the threats that Diamondfield Jack had made against them. It was clearly an attempt by the prosecution to show motive in the killing, and it must have been clear to the jury that Davis was indeed a sworn enemy of sheepmen.

Loren Wilson and Joseph Wilson, the two herders who had been in Dunn's camp the night of February 2, then told the story of how they had been fired upon mysteriously and without provocation. E. R. "Inky" Dayley, the sheepman who had been deputized to go to Arizona after Diamondfield Jack, described how Davis had been returned from the Arizona Penitentiary where he was confined. He also detailed his conversation with Davis on the train, during which Diamondfield Jack claimed that all he knew of the shooting was what

Sparks-Harrell superintendent James E. Bower had told him of it in Wells, Nevada, on or about the sixth of February.

Bower took the stand shortly thereafter to deny that he had had such a conversation with Davis, although he confirmed that he had been with Gleason and Davis on the fifth at the HD ranch and on the sixth in Wells.

The next witness was C. D. Edwards, who was the Sparks-Harrell foreman at the Boar's Nest ranch. He testified that he ate his noon meal at the San Jacinto ranch on the fourth and returned to the Boar's Nest to find Davis and Gleason finishing a meal. Their horses were unsaddled and stabled, and did not appear to have been ridden hard. Although the prosecution had called this witness, he seems to have strengthened the defense position momentarily by reporting the arrival of Davis and Gleason at the Boar's Nest as an early and leisurely one.

Several other Sparks-Harrell men then testified for the prosecution. Bill Trotter described the general lay-out of the ranches. Aaron Critchfield of the San Jacinto reported seeing Frank Smith with a hunting coat he had never seen him wear before, and Harve Tranmer of the Brown ranch testified to the presence of Davis and Gleason there on the second, third, and fourth of February—as well as to witnessing the exchange of coats between Smith and Davis a few days earlier at the Middlestacks.

J. W. Walker, an independent cattleman, testified to meeting Gleason at the Brown ranch early in February of 1896, and to being introduced to a heavily armed

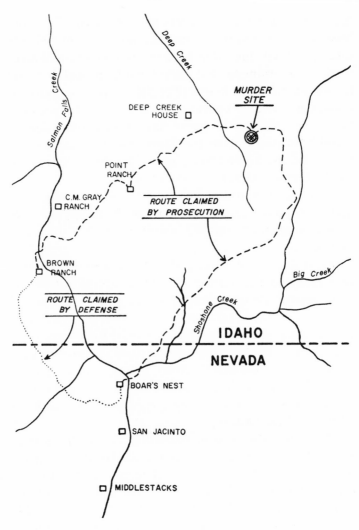

The two disputed routes of Diamondfield Jack's ride, which
became a prime issue at his trial.

stranger named Miller. When he was asked if the defendant in the courtroom was the man he met, Walker said he did not think that he was. As a cowman Walker went on to estimate that horses could probably travel five or six miles per hour under the weather and ground conditions on that February 4. This was the prosecution's first attempt to prove that Davis and Gleason could have ridden from the Brown ranch to the murder scene and back into Nevada in the interval between their observed departure from the Brown ranch and their observed arrival at San Jacinto. Several other men then testified as to the possible speed of the ride, the estimates generally ranging somewhat higher than that of Walker.

Bill Tolman, the Oakley sheepman whom Diamond-field Jack had wounded in November of 1895, took the stand briefly. He was allowed to testify that he had had trouble with Davis on occasion, but not to testify that he had been shot by him. This would have meant the introduction of evidence on a separate and distinct crime. George Porter of Deeth, Nevada, then testified to his conversation with Davis, particularly Jack's damaging statement: "I'm getting forty dollars a month for shooting sheepherders."

The state's star witness was Frank Smith, the former Sparks-Harrell rider. Smith recounted the shooting practice at the Middlestacks, the exchange of coats, and the return of Davis and Gleason on the afternoon of the fourth. The horses looked as if they had been ridden hard, said Smith. He also testified he had overheard Gleason tell Henry Harris that they had indeed been ridden hard. Smith then described his later encounters with Davis, on the twentieth of February when Davis talked about the Deep Creek killing as well as the shooting at the Dunn camp, and on the twenty-fourth when Diamondfield Jack asked him about leaving the country.

James Hawley came back at Smith with a vigorous and embarrassing cross-examination designed to discredit the witness. Smith admitted that he had gone by several names in the past. In the Cherokee Strip of Oklahoma and in New Mexico he had been known as Charley Hill. After fleeing from an assault and battery charge in New Mexico, he went to Arizona as Jim Gordon. Later he went to California where he became Frank Smith. His real name, he admitted, was W. Brummet, Jr. He acknowledged that he had been fired by Sparks-Harrell, and that he had arranged with two other men, McGinty and Lewis, to split the reward if the three of them could see to it that Davis was caught and convicted. Hawley asked several impeaching questions—to determine whether Smith had ever admitted that he really had no knowledge of Davis' guilt—but Smith denied them all. He also denied stealing the letter from Doc Goodin's pocket, the letter that put the authorities onto Gleason's trail.

After a surveyor had testified that the ride would have been some fifty-three or fifty-four miles in length, the final prosecution evidence was introduced to fix the time of Davis' and Gleason's departure from the Brown ranch. Harve Tranmer was recalled to testify that the Brown ranch was deep in a canyon and did not see the sun itself on winter days until late in the afternoon. He reported that the men left shortly after "sun-up," but he admitted that this was an ambiguous expression at the ranch since they had only daylight, not sunlight, by which to judge at that time of the year. An almanac was introduced by the prosecution to fix the time of "sun-up." It was grossly inaccurate, but it went unchallenged—perhaps a tribute to the authority of farmers' almanacs on the frontier. For February 4, 1896, it gave a single time, 7:19 A.M., for sunrise for all of the northern Rocky Mountain states, including Idaho. For Nevada and a group of Southwestern states the time given was 7:02. The inference was that sunrise was shortly after seven. (In reality, on that date in that latitude and longitude according to an accurate ephemeris, the sun rose at 7:50.) But the defense attorneys apparently accepted the evidence from the inaccurate farmers' almanac without protest.

Immediately after the prosecution rested on Monday, April 12, the defense attorneys began presenting their case. Hawley made the opening statement, characterized by the blunt, hard-hitting analysis for which he was famous. He announced essentially that the defense would establish three related facts: that the sheepherders were alive at least until February 4, that Davis was out of the area by mid-day of the fourth, and that the ride required for Davis to have committed the crime in the available time was physically impossible.

On the next day the first defense witness was called. Davis Hunter, the last man to see the sheepherders alive, testified to leaving Wilson and Cummings at breakfast time on the fourth. On his way to Oakley he met two other men on the road, riding together. One was superintendent James E. Bower. The other man he did not know, but he did not think it was Diamondfield Jack or Jeff Gray.

Bower was called again, this time as a defense witness. He said that he and cowboy Jeff Gray had met and were riding together on the range that day near the scene of the murder. He said they had met a man in a cart, a man he later learned was Davis Hunter. Bower and Gray rode on a while and then split up, Bower going to the Point ranch and Gray to Buck Rice's place. Jeff Gray then testified, confirming Bower's story. Hunter and Gray then confronted each other in the courtroom. Neither man was able to identify the other as the man he had met on the road on that occasion, although Bower and Hunter did agree that they recognized each other.

T. M. Gray, father of Jeff, testified that while riding the range that day he had noticed a single set of tracks in the snow leading to the Point ranch, and I. T. Robinson of the Point ranch then confirmed that Bower had indeed been there on the afternoon of the fourth as he had testified.

Henry Harris, the Negro foreman at the Middlestacks, was the next defense witness. He denied Frank Smith's allegation that Beady and the buckskin showed signs of hard riding or that Gleason had said anything about such riding. He judged that the two men were at the Middlestacks by about three or three-thirty that afternoon.

Jeff Gray was recalled to testify to Beady's capabilities, particularly in view of the horse's lameness. "I think he could probably average three miles an hour," he said. "He might have gone 40 or 50 miles a day if he was given time. It would take him ten hours to make it." (In the light of later events, it is interesting to note that cowboy Jeff Gray seemed to be trying to protect Diamondfield Jack.) Gray also reported an interesting conversation with former Sparks-Harrell cowboy Frank Smith in December of 1896 in which Smith told him he had a scheme to make Sparks-Harrell put up "hush money," and to make the company regret that it had fired him.

Several other defense witnesses reported similar experiences with Frank Smith. Carl Domrose said Smith told him that he would make a lot of money out of the case. So did Lester Weatherman and Mike Donahue of Sparks-Harrell. Chester Dwight, Sparks-Harrell cowboy, said Smith had threatened to kill him if he did not corroborate Smith's version of the events at the Middlestacks ranch. Dr. R. D. Roberts and J. E. Comerford of Albion each described a conversation with Smith in which he said that he really knew nothing that would implicate Gleason and Davis. James Walton testified that Smith once told him about stealing the letter from Doc Goodin's pocket at the Shoe Sole ranch late one night. Walton admitted under cross-examination, however, that the only reason he was testifying for the defense was that Smith, Lewis, and McGinty had reneged on a promise to share the reward with him if he testified for the prosecution. Walton may have been a questionable character as a defense witness, but the evidence at this point generally made it look as if Smith, the star witness for the prosecution, was an even less savory character trying to get back at Sparks-Harrell in whatever way he could.

Several of this last group of witnesses also testified to the speed which they thought could be made across the range on cowponies in midwinter, the estimates generally being that about nine or ten hours would have been required for the alleged ride of Davis and Gleason. C. B. Moore, the hotelkeeper from Wells, was the final defense witness. He testified that superintendent Bower, Gleason, and Davis stayed at his establishment on the sixth. On cross-examination he conceded, however, that Gleason and Davis were talking in such a way around town that people thought them guilty of the crime on Deep Creek.

Attorneys Hawley and Perky did not call Diamondfield Jack to testify in his own defense. He was simply too talkative, too unpredictable, to be trusted to face the skillful cross-examination of Borah, Powers, and Rogers.

The evidence was all in. Generally speaking, it showed that Wilson and Cummings had been shot in the wagon by a .44-caliber gun at close range and had been dead for a number of days when their bodies were discovered. Davis was shown to have threatened sheepmen on numerous occasions, but was not shown to have had any dealings with Wilson or Cummings or to have been aware of their presence on the range. Davis was known to have been out of .45-caliber ammunition.

Davis and Gleason were unaccounted for from about eight in the morning until one in the afternoon. The distance they would have had to travel to commit the crime was nearly fifty-five miles. Other people were in the vicinity of Deep Creek at the time; there were several sheep camps nearby, plus several travelers were along the roads, including such reputable figures as James Bower and Jeff Gray. Some identifications which would have cleared things up were not forthcoming; Gray could not identify Hunter, Hunter could not identify Gray, and Walker could not identify Davis as the heavily armed man he had seen with Gleason. Witnesses disagreed as to the condition of Beady and the buckskin horse; Harris and Edwards said they were in good shape, but Frank Smith swore they showed signs of hard riding. Furthermore, considerable difference of opinion existed as to the possibility of the alleged ride. So the evidence seemed highly conflicting, to say the least.

It was April 14—six days after the testimony had begun—and time for the summation speeches, the closing arguments during which the lawyers tried to show the jury how the evidence supported the side which they represented. By tradition and law the prosecution opened the argument, the defense answered, and the prosecution—with the burden of proof—was entitled to the last word. On the afternoon of the fourteenth John C. Rogers opened for the prosecution. That evening K. I. Perky gave the opening argument for the defense. On the following morning James H. Hawley concluded for the defense, and that afternoon O. W.

Powers closed for the prosecution. Borah did not speak, although he did prepare some notes which one of his recent biographers has mistakenly identified as his summation speech.[2]

Each man eloquently reviewed the case and fervently argued the merits of his own interpretation of the evidence. The trial transcript does not contain the summation speeches, so the only sources of information on this part of the trial are brief newspaper accounts. The *Cassia County Times* reported:

> To the disappointment of all court attendants Mr. Borah did not participate in the final arguments. Judge Rogers opened on behalf of the state. He delivered an argumentative, able, and convincing speech. The Judge is always logical and his appeal for the upholding of law and order was a magnificent specimen of forensic oratory.
>
> At the evening session the defendant's cause was presented by Mr. Perky. He took up the evidence piece by piece, and discussed it in a manner creditable to himself and most effectively for his client. He consumed three hours and was accorded the close attention of the jury and all present. Many of his positions were ingenious and his argument was close, connected, and logical. In closing he made a persuasive, adroit, and eloquent appeal for his client's acquittal.
>
> On Thursday forenoon Hon. James H. Hawley of Boise began the closing argument on behalf of Davis. Mr. Hawley was suffering from a serious indisposition, but notwithstanding this he made a powerful argument. He dissected the evidence with the skill of a master, and made strong arguments in favor of his client. He was particularly strong in applying the law to the evidence. His speech was convincing, forcible, and logical. It is the opinion of all who were fortunate enough to hear him that no more effective argument could have been made on behalf of the prisoner, than the one delivered by Mr. Hawley.

Judge O. W. Powers of Salt Lake, renowned as a platform and forensic orator, closed the case for the prosecution. As a polished orator he stands in the front rank. His address was impassioned as well as logical, and his speech added new laurels to his well-established reputation. His speech is considered by many to have had more than ordinary influence upon the jury.[3]

Judge Powers used one dramatic technique in his summation which must have added considerably to his total effect on the jury. Although there was no ballistics evidence introduced during the trial other than the one empty shell, Powers had sent a man out of the courtroom to fire both a .45 and a .44 cartridge in a .45 revolver. The .45 was struck in the center by the firing pin, but the .44 was struck off center. Powers cited this simple test in reminding the jurymen that the empty .44 shell in evidence had been struck well off center.

Powers, the last of the four speakers, concluded at 5:20 P.M. on April 15, 1897. Immediately Judge C. O. Stockslager instructed the jury members in their duties, in the law pertaining to the case, and in certain legal definitions. The jury retired at 7:30 that evening to begin its deliberations.

Although the evidence was completely circumstantial, the jury seemed satisfied. After deliberating for three hours and five minutes the twelve men returned to the courtroom with their verdict. H. R. Cahoon, the foreman, announced the verdict to the judge and to the courtroom: "Guilty of murder in the first degree."

Hawley and Perky were stunned at the verdict. They had not originally considered the prejudice of the people of the eastern part of the county sufficient reason to move for a change of venue before the trial began. The defense attorneys reasoned that since the burden of proof was with the prosecution, there would have to be evidence introduced showing premeditation to kill Wilson, knowledge of his whereabouts by Davis, and Davis' presence at the scene of the crime as a bare minimum of circumstantial evidence to suggest that Davis did the killing. But none of these things had been established. Hawley and Perky had not counted on the willingness of the jury to accept Davis' threats toward sheepmen in general as establishing his premeditation toward Wilson and his knowledge of Wilson's location; neither did they anticipate the jury's willingness to believe in the possibility of the long ride. To the defense lawyers it looked as if the old concept of reasonable doubt as justification for freeing a man had given way to reasonable possibility as justification for conviction.

A week later, on April 24, Judge Stockslager passed sentence on Diamondfield Jack. When he was given the traditional invitation to say something before sentencing, Davis launched into an hour-long tirade against the lack of evidence, the prejudice in the community of Albion, and the injustice of the trial. When on several occasions he touched upon the subject of the Court, a frown from Stockslager brought a quick "Beg pardon, your honor," from Davis. Finally, when the prisoner was finished, Stockslager passed sentence: on the fourth of June, 1897, at the Cassia County jail Jack Davis, alias Diamondfield Jack, was to be hanged by the neck until dead.

NOTES

[1]The trial transcript is the source of all the testimony mentioned in this chapter.

[2]The speech by Borah which was never delivered is quoted in Marian McKenna, *Borah.*

[3]*Cassia County Times,* April 23, 1897.

Prosecution attorney Orlando W. Powers of Salt Lake city was brought in to aid Borah. (Courtesy of Utah State Historical Society)

The chief prosecutor in the murder trial was William E. Borah, later to become U.S. Senator. (From *Colliers,* July 27, 1907)

John G. Rogers, Cassia County prosecutor. (From French's *History of Idaho*)

James H. Hawley, chief defense attorney whose tenacity finally won Diamondfield Jack his freedom. (From *Colliers,* July 27, 1907)

4

The Wheels of Justice Grind Slow

EVEN THOUGH Diamondfield Jack had been sentenced to hang on June 4, 1897, no one really thought that the execution would be carried out on schedule. Cassia County may have been the frontier in some respects in the 1890's, but it had rule of law—and law generally provides for appeals in capital cases.

Defense attorneys Hawley, Perky, and Puckett were disturbed at the way the completely circumstantial case against Davis had been sold to the jury by the prosecution. But they were experienced enough in criminal law to know that their chances of getting the conviction reversed in a higher court were good, particularly now that they knew the kind of evidence and argument they would have to answer. Within a few days after the end of Davis' trial his attorneys took the first step in combatting the judgment, a motion for a new trial.

Shortly after the Diamondfield Jack trial the state tried Fred Gleason at the same April session of district court in Albion.[1] The legal personnel of the trial remained the same as that of the Davis trial, and so did most of the evidence. The only difference was in the charge itself—aiding and abetting the murder of Cummings, instead of Wilson—and in the fact that the state could not show that Gleason had threatened the sheepmen the way Davis had. But it did show that Gleason was with Davis on the fourth of February, 1896. The jury, however, saw things quite the opposite from the way the Davis jury had seen them. Perhaps because he was a local boy, they acquitted Fred Gleason.

Hawley was probably not surprised by this action. On the contrary, it only confirmed his growing belief that Diamondfield Jack had become the object of the vengeance of the Albion sheepmen and that they wanted his scalp only. Gleason's acquittal might even strengthen Davis' chances with a new trial or a higher court, since the man who had allegedly been with Diamondfield Jack at the scene of the murder had now been cleared.

Perhaps the prosecution lawyers recognized this fact, for they tried again to convict Gleason for the other murder. An information was filed against him for the murder of Wilson, but the case was eventually dismissed when several key witnesses could not be located. Doc Goodin, the Sparks-Harrell cowboy, was supposed to testify that Gleason had admitted to him in Fischer's saloon in Wells that he was with Diamondfield Jack when he killed Wilson and Cummings. But Goodin had disappeared. So had Alice Woods, the madam from Wells, who was slated to report the damaging admissions the two cowboys allegedly had made in her establishment.

With the motion for the new trial pending, Hawley and his two associates began the long and tedious job of gathering and sifting all the information which could possibly aid their case. There seemed to be four avenues worth exploring. First was the possible bias of the jurors; second was the ballistics evidence pertaining to the .44 cartridges in the .45 revolver; third was the possibility that the two men were killed *after* February 4; and fourth, and perhaps most important, was the question of the ride which the prosecution convinced the jury that Davis had made.

Hawley ignored a fifth possibility—the fact that Frank Smith, the chief prosecution witness, had been so thoroughly discredited. R. F. McGinty, the self-styled sheepmen's detective who was to have split the reward with Smith and Lewis, furnished Hawley with an affidavit saying that on numerous occasions he had heard Smith threaten to kill Diamondfield Jack if he were acquitted. On one occasion, in the presence of district attorney Rogers, Smith had said he would like to kill defense attorney Perky as well.

Exploring the first of the four possible approaches, Perky was able to locate several Cassia County women who swore that they had heard one or more of the jurors express a belief in Diamondfield Jack's guilt before the trial began. In the first of literally hundreds of affidavits which were to be submitted by both sides, a Mary Gordon swore that juror George Gray had said he thought Davis was guilty. Mrs. Maria Hagan confirmed that this statement had been made by juror Gray and swore that another juror, George T. Moore, had expressed a similar opinion. Mrs. Lou Robinson also deposed to hearing Gray's statement, and Mrs. Dora Heed swore that her niece, Addie Gordon, had reported the same experience. Mrs. Clara Cureton said she heard juror Stephen Mahoney express the opinion that Diamondfield Jack was guilty before the trial.

So the defense now had some ammunition with which to open its campaign for a new trial. But through the next few months the prosecution answered with affidavits of its own. Jurors Gray and Mahoney swore that the affidavits against them were untrue. District attorney Rogers reported that juror Moore had moved from the county shortly after the trial and could not be found, but he was able to get three affidavits affirming Moore's character and veracity—as well as eight such statements for juror Gray and seven for Mahoney. So, as is often the case, the counter-affidavits of one side tended to nullify the force of the original affidavits.

Round two of the deposition fight ended in a similar standoff. Several men had run some tests for the defense in which they fired a number of .44 cartridges in a .45 revolver. They signed affidavits reporting that the shells frequently ruptured. This evidence would help the defense show that the shell found at the scene of the murder could not have been fired in a .45—and Davis carried a .45—since it had not expanded or ruptured. But within a few months the prosecution came back with affidavits of its own covering similar tests; on this occasion, of course, the discharged shells had not ruptured in any appreciable number. So, again, neither side gained any advantage from the additional tests and affidavits.

Some of the cattlemen had suggested to defense attorney Hawley the possibility that the sheepmen had been killed after February 4, 1896—perhaps by rival sheepmen whose camps were close by. Hawley was not convinced, but in order to leave open the possibility of later using this argument he located a doctor who was willing to swear that the dogs could not have stayed alive for thirteen days tied to the wagon wheel without food or water. The implication here was that the dogs had been free until a much later date than the fourth, and since Davis' whereabouts were well established after the fourth he could not have done the killing. But Borah cleverly countered this argument by statements from two doctors to the effect that dogs could indeed stay alive as long as thirteen days without food and water.

The final issue was the possibility of the ride allegedly made from the Brown ranch to the murder site and back to the Boar's Nest ranch. Testimony in the trial had differed considerably on this point, and all of it was admittedly hypothetical and a matter of opinion. No one really knew if the ride could be made, or had been made within the time limit involved. After the trial both sides were curious but cautious about whether it could be done. The defense made the first move to find out.

On August 24, 1897, George P. Rowberry, a Sparks-Harrell rider, rode the full route. He used two of the company's better horses, riding Comanche to the Point ranch where he changed to Iron Head. Without stopping at the scene of the murder he swung on south into Nevada, reaching the Boar's Nest in five and a half hours. The ride was satisfactory to the defense attorneys, so Rowberry signed an affidavit describing the conditions of the ride. He reported that the second horse was "jaded" and would not feed afterwards. Travel conditions were excellent, he said, but to make the same ride in winter time would probably require eight or eight and a half hours.

Two days later cowboy Jeff Gray tried the same ride for Hawley. Using Casey, another of the top Sparks-Harrell horses, Gray made the ride in five and three quarter hours and stopped more than two miles short of the Boar's Nest. He, too, swore that his horse was exhausted.

Hawley evaluated his position. The testimony in the trial had shown that Davis and Gleason were not seen from about eight in the morning (assuming that "sun-up" comes at that time in early February to a house in a deep canyon in southern Idaho) until shortly after one in the afternoon, a period of about five hours. Two witnesses had reported that Beady and the buckskin did not look tired when Davis and Gleason arrived back in Nevada, and only the unreliable Frank Smith had claimed that the horses showed hard riding. Moreover, Beady had recently been lame; Gray had said the horse would average only three miles an hour. Now the 1897 test with Rowberry and Gray showed that under ideal summer conditions at least five and a half hours of hard riding was necessary to make the fifty-five-mile trip, and that the horses clearly showed the results of it. It simply did not seem possible that Davis and Gleason could have made the ride which the jury believed they made.

On this basis Hawley decided to issue a challenge. In September of 1897 he wrote to District Attorney Rogers proposing that a test ride be made to settle the question of the possibility of the alleged ride, once and for all. He offered to let the prosecution pick the horses and riders, and to allow the riders to practice over the area to get acquainted with it. The defense was even willing to pay good wages to the riders so selected. All that he asked, said Hawley, was the right to place observers at key spots along the route.

Prosecutors Rogers and Borah sensed that they were being maneuvered by the shrewd defense attorney. They did not acknowledge the challenge until they had had time to make their own secret test ride.[2] Inky Dayley, the sheepman, tried the trip in October, but apparently the prosecutors were not satisfied with his time of five hours and ten minutes, particularly since there were no corroborating witnesses. So they planned a test ride for November 12, using three men. But defense attorneys Hawley and Perky got wind of the test and were able to get people spotted at important positions along the route. Billy Majors and Charles Edwards were at the Brown ranch, Mrs. Lou Robinson was at the Point ranch, and William Vail and Lester Weatherman watched the murder site.

The affidavits which each side filed as a result of this test ride told conflicting stories. The three riders, Job Howells, Frank Smith, and Charles Wilson, all swore they made the ride from the Brown ranch past the murder scene and all the way to the Middlestacks ranch —ten miles beyond the Boar's Nest—in four hours and forty-eight minutes. But Majors and Edwards swore that no one left the Brown ranch that morning; they themselves remained until nine o'clock when they left for the Boar's Nest, arriving there in time to see the three riders go by. Mrs. Robinson reported that by standing on a fence she was able to see three men riding by the Point ranch. They were some distance away, off the road rather than on it, but she could see that they were coatless and that one man had a black bandana around his head. She checked the time afterwards and found that it was 7:45 A.M. This contradicted Job Howells who in his affidavit had said that they left the Brown ranch at 7:48 A.M. Weatherman and Vail confirmed the fact that the three coatless riders, one of them with a black bandana around his head, had gone by the murder scene at 9:15 that morning, and had even taken some seven minutes there to adjust their saddles. The men were riding hard and fast since the roads and trails were in good shape.

It now looked as if Hawley had discovered a weakness in the prosecution position. The discrepancies in the two accounts of the test ride seemed significant; the three men apparently had started from the wrong ranch, cutting the length of the ride considerably. Encouraged, the defense attorney waited for prosecutors Rogers and Borah to reply to the challenge for the once-and-for-all test. Finally in December Rogers acknowledged Hawley's letter. But, since he had nothing to gain from the test ride, Rogers declined the invitation of the defense, pointing out that the proper time to have introduced the test ride as evidence was during the original trial. It was a frustrating moment for the hopes of the defense.

Another blow to these hopes was struck by Judge C. O. Stockslager. In January of 1898 he overruled the motion for a new trial. Immediately Hawley filed two concurrent appeals with the Idaho Supreme Court, one from Stockslager's denial of the new trial and the other from the original judgment of conviction. The battle of the depositions during the previous six months finally began to pay dividends to the defense. Hawley was able to put together an impressive set of arguments and evidence to support his motion.

Many of the depositions and affidavits were forwarded to the court. One which looked like it would be quite helpful was sworn by Andrew Gray, the brother of Jeff Gray. He said that while searching for horses on the west side of the Salmon Falls River on the morning of February 4, 1896, he saw two men riding south on the Toano road—one on a dark colored horse and one on a lighter one. Gray remembered the event because they were the only men that he saw out on the range during the entire winter. Fred Gleason had earlier deposed to seeing a man near the Toano road on the day he and Davis claimed they rode south from the Brown ranch on the bay horse Beady and the buckskin. This was the first confirmation of their alibi.

Hawley's motion for a new trial had six points, most of which dealt with routine procedural matters in the courtroom. Two points dealt with evidence, one saying that the verdict was contrary to the evidence and the other saying that new evidence had since been discovered—the test ride—which was not available at the original trial. In support of these points regarding evidence Hawley assigned a long list of errors in the original trial.

These included the fact that Diamondfield Jack was not shown to be present at the crime; that the evidence did not show when murder victim Wilson had been shot or when he died; that the evidence suggested the wounding took place *after* February 4, 1896, and that Davis was shown to be elsewhere; that the horse ride was shown to be physically impossible; that no motive was shown; that no intent to kill, or even a knowledge of Wilson's existence or presence was shown; that no malice was shown; that guilt beyond reasonable doubt was not shown; that Davis was not shown to have a gun capable of inflicting the fatal wound; and that no evidence of threats against Wilson and Cummings had been shown. It was an imposing argument; although there were a few weak points there were also some rather telling points which certainly raised the question of reasonable doubt. In addition, Hawley cited other procedural errors in the admission of certain testimony and in the alleged misconduct of the jury.

The original trial transcript was printed in book form and filed, along with Hawley's legal brief, with the Idaho Supreme Court in March of 1898.[3] There were two interesting sidelights to the printing of the transcript. One was the fact that the printing job was awarded to C. B. Steunenberg, publisher of the Albion *Times* and brother of Frank Steunenberg, the influential printer-turned-sheepman who happened to be governor of Idaho at the time. Second was the fact that the transcript was edited or abstracted; instead of being recorded in the traditional form of actual question and answer, the answers were reworked to include the questions. Thus, the answers that a man gave to a long series of questions appeared in the transcript as a single, long—and somewhat disconnected—statement. This made it rather difficult for any subsequent reader of the transcript, including the Supreme Court justices, to get exact shades of meaning from the testimony.

In addition to the ambiguity created by this kind of transcript, another questionable technique further complicated the job of understanding what had happened during the trial. Certain rather important ideas were inked in on the typewritten transcript sent to the printer—by whom, nobody knows. But they definitely changed the meaning, and they changed it in favor of the prosecution. For example, when Harve Tranmer was describing the shooting contests at the Middlestacks ranch in late January, 1896, he said that Davis was out of .45 cartridges. The transcript that went to the printer was altered, in ink, to read: "He said he was shooting .44's." Also, at one point when Jeff Gray was talking about the horse Beady, the transcript has him saying, "At the time I turned him over Beady could not make 8 or 10 miles for one hour." The word *not* had been inked out, completely changing the meaning in favor of the prosecution again. Perhaps these changes reflect only sloppy work in compiling the transcript and getting it to the printer, but there is also the possibility that the transcript was deliberately edited to favor the prosecution.

In any event, the Idaho Supreme Court justices spent several months with the transcript and announced their decision on June 15, 1898. It was a staggering blow to Diamondfield Jack. On both appeals the high court supported Judge Stockslager. In a lengthy decision the court answered Hawley's legal points.[4]

In essence, the decision said that the evidence *did* support the conviction, that the killing was on or about February 4, that motive and premeditation were shown, that Davis was shown to be using .44 cartridges in a .45, that Davis had threatened sheepmen as a class of people. The court cited the numerous threats which the sheepmen had described. It said the evidence showed deliberate planning and preparation of an alibi; circumstances and actions of the defendant pointed to Davis and Gleason as the parties who attacked sheepherders Wilson and Cummings. The court also said there was no attempt by the defense to show that Davis and Gleason were anywhere else; the impossibility of the ride was their only alibi, and the jury had believed the ride could be done.

On the procedural errors the court also had much to say. Hawley had argued that deputized sheepman Inky Dayley's conversation with Davis while bringing him back from Arizona was inadmissible. During the trial Dayley had testified that Diamondfield Jack told him that he had learned of the killing about the sixth of

February from superintendent James E. Bower. The court ruled the conversation was admissible because it showed guilty knowledge since the crime was not discovered until the sixteenth of February.

Another rebuff came on the question of the biased jurors. The high court ruled that because each juror had sworn, during his initial examination in the jury selection process, that he was unbiased, this was sufficient proof of his lack of bias. It said,

> It would be a dangerous practice to establish the rule that the verdict of a jury, which is fully sustained by the evidence, should be set aside on the ground that one or two *ex parte* affidavits are presented to the effect that one of the individual jurors had expressed an opinion prior to the trial to the effect that the accused is guilty, but which statement is denied by the juror, who is proven to be a man of good reputation for truth and veracity.[5]

The decision was truly discouraging to Hawley. The court had accepted the prosecution explanation of each bit of circumstantial evidence in every respect. Reasonable doubt had gone down the drain. Without much hope, Hawley filed for a rehearing. Predictably, the court denied it to him. Diamondfield Jack's situation was becoming critical for the first time.

In Idaho the state Board of Pardons served as a kind of court-of-last-resort. It was a three-man board made up of the governor, the secretary-of-state, and the attorney general. Their powers were broad in both pardons and appeals, exceeding in some respects those of the Supreme Court. Hawley now turned to this group in a last-ditch effort to keep his client alive. On July

25, 1898, he filed an application for a pardon. He was granted a hearing for mid-October. But in September the Supreme Court resentenced Davis to hang on October 21. Obviously, the pardon board hearing now became literally a matter of life and death for the young cowboy.

And what of Diamondfield Jack in the meantime? He had been confined to the Cassia County jail in Albion for almost a year and a half. Reportedly he had once gone "over the hill" during this time but was retaken in a Nevada saloon without resistance.[6] He had watched the legal proceedings from his jail cell with some interest, but now he was impatient and angry with the way things were going for him. Attorney K. I. Perky had the thankless job of placating Davis. With the cooperation of the jailers he was generally able to show the curious people of Albion a model prisoner, but there were moments when Perky had to stand the full brunt of Davis' bitter tongue. The cowboy accused his lawyers of deserting him, of botching up his defense, of keeping him quiet in the courtroom when he should have been standing up telling the truth. This last point was the one that rubbed salt into the lawyer's wounds, because if Diamondfield Jack had only done less talking from the beginning, he would not have been in trouble at the moment. Besides, he simply didn't know what the word truth meant!

"He is the most disagreeable client to manage I ever came in contact with," Perky wrote to Hawley. On several occasions he reported to his legal associate that the prisoner was crazy or demented. "He also has an idea that he is a man of destiny—and firmly believes that he will lead a revolution in Mexico, and divide the Mexican republic with President Díaz."[7] Obviously, it would be a tough job to sell the pardon board on the idea that Davis should go free, particularly if the board chose to interview the talkative prisoner.

Perky had been doing a good deal of detective work in Cassia County during this time. He knew that Diamondfield Jack had been hired as a gunman by the cattle company, and that Gleason and Majors had worked in a similar capacity. So he had no illusions about the kind of man his client was. But as he prowled around, sifting facts and opinions in Cassia County, he had a growing conviction that Jack Davis had not killed the two sheepherders. Several key Sparks-Harrell men such as Joe Langford and Doc Goodin—men who seemed to have inside information—had vanished; some kind of chicanery seemed afoot, and it was being concealed from the Sparks-Harrell attorneys. Frank Smith had even sworn to the pardon board that Goodin was paid $1,000 by Sparks to drop from sight.

In Boise, James Hawley sat reviewing the evidence, slowly arriving at the same conclusion. A week after the Supreme Court decision he wrote a challenge to his employer, John Sparks. "Is it not time," asked Hawley, "the persons who killed the sheep men made open announcement of the fact? It strikes me they should speak and take their chances."[8] But cattle-baron Sparks remained tight-lipped, and did not acknowledge the cryptic and daring challenge.

A few brave and free-thinking Cassia County residents were also publicly skeptical of Davis' guilt. In August J. M. Pierce wrote to the pardon board saying that the guilty men were in the county and would soon be found. In September the new editor of the Albion *Cassia County Times,* Charles S. Mark, editorialized that the pardon board should commute the sentence. That same month Lewis Sweetser told the board that Davis' reputation, not his guilt, was what really convicted him. Hardy Sears pointed out that Gleason was acquitted on the same evidence that had convicted Davis; he also ventured the opinion that the majority of people in the county now had doubts about the verdict. Several other people wrote the board in a similar vein, including Sheriff O. P. Anderson, who cited the dogs and the ride as his reasons for believing Davis innocent. The sheriff also said he thought the guilty ones would soon be caught.

But the prosecution, sensing a possible change in public opinion, was also busy reinforcing its position. Late in 1897 an affidavit had been sworn by Randolph Streeter of Lamoille, Nevada, which prosecutor Borah seemed to think was quite important. Streeter had said that Davis told him of a shooting scrape with some Idaho sheepmen, during which he had ridden up to a herder's camp and shot two men. There was no mention of killing, just shooting, but Davis had told him he was getting $150 or $200 a month for patrolling the cattle range.

While this statement did not seem like a particularly incriminating bit of evidence, quite a battle of affidavits developed around it. Streeter's stepfather deposed that the boy had a weak character, was drunk at the time the affidavit was signed, and that the young man had never claimed to have heard Davis admit the killing of a sheepherder. Borah produced other affidavits to show that Streeter was not drunk at the time. He also managed to turn up an affidavit from a Thomas Short, who was in the Gheen store in Lamoille Valley the night that Diamondfield Jack boasted of shooting sheepherders; Short swore that Davis claimed to have shot Cummings, one of the two murder victims. While the Short affidavit may have hurt Diamondfield Jack, the furor over the Streeter affidavit did not, for finally Randolph Streeter sent an affidavit to the Idaho pardon board saying specifically that Davis had told him only of the earlier incident in which he had wounded sheepman Bill Tolman, and the other occasion when he had exchanged shots with the Wilson brothers at the Dunn sheepcamp near Point ranch.

As time grew near for the October pardon board hearing, defense attorneys Hawley and Perky rode the cattle trails of Cassia County, trying to turn up the one lead that would break the log jam of conjecture in their own minds. Both men were suspicious; the cattlemen of the area seemed to be sticking together as tightly as the sheepmen. Somewhere the truth was being suppressed.

After repeatedly going over the evidence, Hawley kept coming back to one fact: Davis Hunter, the last man to see the herders alive, had testified that he met two riders shortly after leaving the sheep camp. During the trial, superintendent James E. Bower and Jeff Gray had admitted that they were the men whom Hunter encountered that day. This placed them closer to the murder scene than anyone else, and considerably closer than Davis and Gleason. Then there was that conversation on the train in Nevada reported by the deputized sheepman, Dayley: Diamondfield Jack had claimed that Bower mentioned the shooting of the two herders to him in Wells on the sixth of February. The Supreme Court had interpreted this as meaning that Davis knew of the crime that early because he had committed it himself, but the judges had missed the point—Bower really did tell Davis, because Bower knew of the crime!

Early in September of 1898 Hawley wrote to the superintendent, accusing him of being involved in the crime and asking that he come forth and admit that Diamondfield Jack was innocent. With the hanging of Diamondfield Jack only a month away, James E. Bower summoned his courage and made a remarkable deposition.

NOTES

[1]Most of the facts of this chapter, including the results of the Gleason trial, are reconstructed from the large number of depositions submitted to the pardon board from 1897 until 1899.

[2]Borah ordered the secret ride in a letter to the secretary of the local wool growers association, dated October 19, 1897. The letter is preserved in the Borah collection of the Idaho Historical Society.

[3]The Hawley papers of the Idaho Historical Society include the typed version of the transcript; the printed version is filed with the Idaho Supreme Court.

[4]The Supreme Court decision is *State* v. *Davis,* 53 Pacific 678.

[5]*State* v. *Davis,* 53 Pacific 678.

[6]The reference to Davis' absence from jail is in a letter to the author from Mrs. Margaret A. Peterson of Seattle, Washington, granddaughter of Deputy Sheriff Quinn.

[7]Perky's comments about Davis are contained in letters to James Hawley dated October 29, 1897, and December 2, 1897.

[8]Hawley's letter to Sparks, dated June 22, 1898, is in the Hawley papers. Sparks' correspondence to Hawley is written in a virtually illegible longhand, and throws no light onto the relationship between client and attorney.

Defense attorney Kirtland I. Perky, whose detective work led to the Bower-Gray confessions. (Courtesy of Idaho State Historical Society)

Superintendent James E. Bower, one of the two men who finally admitted their role in the shootings. (From French's *History of Idaho*)

The Cassia County courthouse in Albion, Idaho, scene of the murder trial of Diamondfield Jack. (From the *Idaho Statesman,* March 13, 1938)

5

The Bower-Gray Story

State of Idaho ⎱
County of Cassia ⎰ ss

James E. Bower being first duly sworn deposes and says:

I am now and have for more than twenty-five years past been a resident of Cassia County, Idaho, and during that time have been and now am engaged in the business of farming and stock-growing. On the 4th day of February, 1896, I was and for several years prior thereto had been, in addition to my business as farmer and stockgrower, in the employ of the Sparks Harrell Cattle Company as Superintendent. Said company has extensive holdings of land in Idaho and Nevada including ranches near and on Rock Creek, at Deep Creek, at the Point and at various places on and near Salmon Falls River in Idaho, and also on that portion of the Salmon River in Nevada and extending from the head of the Salmon to Tecoma on the Central Pacific Railroad. Said company had also a great many cattle upon the ranges contiguous to said ranches, a part of their range being in the vicinity of Deep Creek and also of Shoshone Basin in

Cassia County. My business as Superintendent required me to make frequent trips to the various ranches of the company, and upon the ranges adjacent thereto.

In the latter part of January, 1896, I went from Kelton, Utah, to Albion for the purpose of securing at the latter place adoption papers for my stepdaughter, Eva Thomas. She was about to be married in Ogden where she was then staying with her mother, my wife, and it had been arranged to have the wedding on February 10. Eva was always known by my name, and both my wife and myself earnestly desired that she be formally adopted by me, so that she could be married as my daughter and by my Christian name.

Upon reaching Albion, which I did on January 31, I consulted K. I. Perky, Esq., upon the matter and was informed by him that owing to Eva's absence from Albion I could not secure the adoption papers, but that I could secure them in Ogden just as well as at Albion.

The Sparks-Harrell Company had an important law suit pending at Elko, Nevada, which had been set for hearing on February 12, and the witnesses for the company were on Salmon River. It was part of my duty to notify these witnesses of the pendency of this action and secure their attendance at the trial. I also had a shipment of cattle to make from Reno, Nevada, on the 6th or 7th of February. I also had some private business of importance to attend to at my ranch on Dry Creek, about 35 miles from Albion. It was impossible for me to attend to these matters at the times mentioned without my riding from Albion by way of my Dry Creek ranch and from there to Salmon River and thence to Wells, Nevada, a distance of about 190 miles. It was impossible for me to make this trip at that time with my team, the way I generally travelled, and I resolved to go on horseback.

I went to Dry Creek from Albion on February 1, and on the evening of the 2nd went to Rock Creek. I was feeding about 1,500 head of cattle at different places on Rock Creek which demanded my attention and this occupied my time until the evening of the 3rd.

On the morning of February 4th, between 8 and 9 o'clock, I left Rock Creek on horseback intending to go to Salmon River that day. I wore over my ordinary clothes a heavy fur overcoat. I had a pistol which I carried in a scabbard hung from my left shoulder and under my ordinary coat.

Prior to this time considerable ill feeling had been engendered between cattle and sheep men over the range in the vicinity of Deep Creek, and also in Shoshone Basin. There had several years before been an understanding between the two classes of stockgrowers, by the terms of which the cattle men were to abandon the range east of the Goose Creek Divide and the sheep men were not to interfere with the range on the west of the divide which included Deep Creek and Shoshone Basin. This agreement had been observed by both parties until a year or so before the date of my trip, but so many bands of sheep from Utah had been driven upon the ranges used by the sheepmen in Cassia County that they had become overstocked, and many herds had more or less infringed on the range reserved for the cattle men.

Rock Creek and vicinity is settled almost entirely by persons who in addition to farming carry on the business of cattle raising, their herds all ranging together with the cattle of the Sparks-Harrell Company on the range west of the Goose Creek divide.

Some trouble had occurred between the two classes, by reason of the matters mentioned, in the summer and fall of 1895. The sheep men had not only, as before stated, infringed upon the cattlemen's range, but had in many instances trespassed upon fenced fields of the settlers. They were in the habit of going thoroughly armed, and many threats against myself and other cattle men were reported.

It was reported to me early in January, 1896, that an organized effort was being made by owners of sheep ranging north of Snake River in Lincoln County, and who did not live in the State of Idaho, to drive all their herds upon the range occupied by the cattle men in Cassia County, and so make it impossible for cattle to range there longer.

A man by the name of Wm. Vail had been living upon Rock Creek, and stopping with cattle men there during the year 1895. For various reasons, all of which I now think were unfounded, the cattle men, or many of them at least— myself included, had become suspicious of Vail and imagined he was in communication with the sheep men and betraying the cattle men.

After starting from Rock Creek on the morning of February 4, 1896, as before stated, I rode on alone for about 2½ miles and was then overtaken by Jeff Gray who was also on horseback. Jeff informed me that he was going to Buck Rice's place to see about gathering some horses. Jeff Gray had not been in the company employ during the time I had charge of affairs, and I had not to my knowledge seen him for several weeks. I was surprised when he overtook me, as I had no idea of meeting him and did not know he was in that section of country.

A horseman had been ahead of me from the time I had left Rock Creek. He was riding hard and I did not positively identify him, but thought it was Wm. Vail. After Jeff overtook me we rode along together. I called his attention to the horseman ahead, who several times appeared in sight as he was crossing high points of the country. He also thought it was Vail.

Jeff Gray and I rode along together until we reached a point near Buck Rice's ranch and there ascertained by reason of the absence of tracks in the light covering of snow that Rice was not at home. Jeff then concluded to go on with me as far as the Point ranch.

About two miles from Rice's ranch the Shoshone road leading up to Deep Creek leaves the main road to Rock Creek. The distance to Point ranch is about the same by either road.

At Goat Springs about 2½ miles from Buck Rice's ranch Gray and I had met a man driving a cart. He was a stranger to both of us at the time, although I have since ascertained his name is Davis Hunter. He was evidently a sheep man, and I thought by reason of my not knowing him that he was a stranger. My mind at once reverted back to the rumors I had heard in regard to the sheep men north of Snake River being about to overrun the Deep Creek and Shoshone Basin ranges; this, in connection with the horseman ahead whom I supposed was Vail and who by his hard riding showed he did not wish to be overtaken, caused me considerable anxiety, as I was afraid the sheep men's threats were being carried out and that the suspicions we had in regard to Vail were being verified.

After reaching the parting of the roads we found the cart tracks came from the direction of two sheep camps that were there in sight. I looked for the tracks of the horseman who had been ahead of us and they were no longer in the road. I concluded therefore he had gone to the sheep camps.

The nearest of these camps was I should judge about a quarter mile from the road we had been travelling and was on the east side of Deep Creek, upon the hill; the other camp was, I should think, from ½ to ¾ of a mile distant.

Wishing to see if my idea about Vail was correct and also to ascertain whether the camps had been moved from north of Snake River, I rode over to the nearest camp accompanied by Gray. We rode up in front of the wagon and dismounted, each of us throwing our bridles over our horses heads to the ground. I should think it was about 30 feet from the wagon where we dismounted. Gray had a rifle on his saddle but did not take it or unloosen it in any way. The flap of the wagon cover was open. A man came to the front of the wagon and I said, "Hello, are you getting dinner?" The man said yes. Gray and I both got into the wagon and sat down on the side board near the front of the wagon. This wagon was like the ordinary sheepman's wagon, a bed in the back end of it, a board running along the entire length where things could be placed or a person could sit, and a small cooking stove on the right hand side as you got in and near the front.

When we got in the wagon I saw another man near the bed. There was a fire in the stove and they evidently were cooking dinner. It was then I should judge between 11 and 12 o'clock. Gray sat down next to the end of the wagon and between the front of the wagon and myself. I had my heavy overcoat on and had it buttoned up when I sat down. I did not know either of the men, and not recognizing them I concluded they were parties that had come from the north side of Snake River, and were not residents of the county.

After sitting down I said in my ordinary tone and not in a loud, menacing or offensive manner, "Do you think it is right to come in here with your sheep?" The man in front of the wagon said, "We have as much right in here as anyone." I said, "I don't think you have. You don't pay any taxes in this county." The same man said, "We do pay taxes here." I said, "I think you are mistaken about that." Up to this time the conversation had been in an ordinary tone upon both sides. I was not angry and didn't suppose the other parties were. As I made the last remark the man in front said, "You are a lying son of a bitch," speaking loudly and angrily, and jumped to his feet from where he was sitting nearly opposite me, and started for me. I jumped to my feet, and as I did so saw Jeff Gray getting out of the wagon; as I got up I started to step back but the man who had been doing the talking grabbed me by the collar and shoulder and threw me back over the end gate of the wagon. He may have struck me, but I don't know positively. As he threw me the end gate struck me across the small of the back, my head and shoulders being over the end and outside of the wagon and my legs inside. He kept on me, bearing me out. I grappled with him but he was the stoutest and could easily manage me in the position I was in. I was considerably dazed by the onslaught made upon me, and was satisfied that I was about to suffer great bodily injury. I recollected having my pistol inside my undercoat and as two buttons had been torn off my overcoat I reached for my pistol and got hold of it. The man on me grasped it also and said something about fixing me, and had the pistol about away from me, when I heard a shot which seemed to have been fired close to my head. I saw a wound, or at least blood, on his chin as I heard the shot fired. He relaxed his hold on the pistol as soon as the shot was fired, and upon me also, and I turned my head and saw Jeff standing on the ground near the head of the wagon and a little to the right. He was in the act of raising and, as I supposed, cocking his pistol. I said to him "hold on" and he didn't shoot again. The man who was on me had relaxed his hold but was leaning heavily on me, and apparently becoming helpless. He was bleeding from the wound on the chin and the blood was dropping on me. I raised both him and myself up, and as I did so he said, "I am badly hurt." I said, "I don't think you are," and I helped him over on the bed. The other man was standing at the head of the bed. He said nothing during all of this time. Nothing more was said as I got out of the wagon as quick as possible. I saw Gray as I got out standing a few feet away putting some cartridges in his pistol. We at once got on our horses and started away from the wagon toward Deep Creek. I said to Jeff, "We had better go and tell these other parties (meaning the other camp) about this trouble." Jeff said, "No, they have heard or seen us and we may get into more trouble." We went on to Deep Creek and in going over I said to Jeff, "This is a serious thing. With all the trouble that has been going on, we will be blamed for this trouble." Jeff said, "No, these other fellows will be after us in less than half an hour."

We were on Deep Creek by this time and I said to Jeff that I was going on to the railroad and he could do as he pleased. He said he was going back to Rock Creek. We then parted and I rode as fast as I could to the Point ranch, stopped there a short time and rode on to the Brown ranch on Salmon. I expected trouble on the road, because so many threats had been made against me, that I believed if I had been recognized as one of the parties to the difficulty a mob of the sheep men would follow me and kill me. The next day I went to the Vineyard ranch, saw my witnesses for the Elko suit and the next day went to the H. D. ranch for dinner and went on to Wells that night, and on the morning of the 7th went to Reno to load the cattle.

While I was sitting in the wagon I was smoking a corn cob pipe that I had purchased that morning at Tatro's store on Rock Creek, and when I was assaulted the force used caused the pipe to drop out of my mouth.

I heard but one shot fired during the affray, although I know more were fired, as Gray told others who told me long afterwards that he had fired several times. After I got out of the wagon Gray said, "I didn't shoot until he got hold of your gun and had about got it away from you, and knew they would kill us both."

I discovered after getting to the Point ranch that my watch chain had been broken in the affray and the guard was gone.

I did not have, when I went to the wagon or into it, the slightest idea of a difficulty, and if I had had such idea would not have gone there. When we left the sheep wagon I did not believe that the man who had hold of me was badly shot as the wound seemed to be in the face and I knew of no other wound. The second man I did not think was hurt at all, but I believed he was badly frightened. My impression was, and I think it was Gray's also, that the parties with whom we had the difficulty would very quickly alarm the other sheep men in the vicinity and we would be pursued and mobbed, as I had been threatened often. I saw no mention of the affair in the papers for over two weeks, and that made me feel certain no one had been badly hurt.

When I reached the H. D. ranch on February 6, I met Jack Davis and Fred Gleason there and they rode into Wells with me. This was the first time I had seen or heard from either of them for over two weeks. Neither of them had any connection with the killing of Wilson and Cummings or were privy to it in any way.

After the bodies of Wilson and Cummings were found my first impression was to tell the whole matter as it occurred, but excitement was running high and so many threats had been made that I was satisfied that if I did so that both Gray and myself would be murdered. After Davis and Gleason were arrested, I desired to speak and relate the whole matter, but the same conditions still prevailed, and as I did not believe it possible for innocent men to be convicted of a serious crime, I remained silent waiting for a more opportune moment to make a full statement. After the Supreme Court had decided against Jack Davis's motion for a new trial and he had been resentenced, I realized that an innocent man was about to be hanged for a crime in regard to which he had not the slightest knowledge, and then resolved to make public my knowledge of the affair. I sent word to Jeff Gray by Henry Jones, his brother-in-law, on Monday, October 3, 1898, that I was going to Boise and that the true story of the killing of Wilson and Cummings had to be told, that he could go to Boise with me or take care of himself, that Jack Davis should not hang. The next day Mr. Jones told me that Jeff had told him to tell me to do as I thought best. I went at once to Boise and gave a full statement of the affair to Hawley & Puckett, attorneys for Davis.

I heard soon after this affray that Jeff Gray had told Buck Rice all about it. I met Rice and Jeff together about two months after and made a statement of the affair to him, and he told me that I had stated it exactly as had Jeff Gray. Jeff was present during our conversation.

Complaints have been made against me, charging me with the murder of both Wilson and Cummings. I was taken before Justice Hansen of Rock Creek on October 12, and had my examination and on this day have been held to answer before the next term of the District Court and my bail fixed at ten thousand dollars which I have given.

(s) James E. Bower

Subscribed and sworn to before me this 13th day of October, 1898. Lawrence Hansen, Justice of the Peace.[1]

Here was a startling development, and the first real break in the two-and-a-half-year-old case! Admitting his presence at the murder of the two sheepherders was one of the most respected and solid citizens of Cassia County. Bower was no saddle tramp; he was the man who had built the first schoolhouse in the area and the man who organized the first Sunday school classes. Born in Ohio in 1854, he had spent his boyhood in Missouri until, at age 15, he went to Wyoming on a cattle drive. Although he had little formal education, in his years in Idaho he had risen above the level of a cowboy to become a Sparks-Harrell superintendent as well as an independent cattleman. He became a gentleman—as witnessed by the impeccable handwriting, language, and grammar of his written confession quoted above—in a land singularly short of gentlemen. And yet he had been involved in a range murder.

On the same day that Bower made his confession, Jeff Gray signed an affidavit confirming in every detail the story told by Bower. He added additional details explaining how he had been pushed out of the wagon, and had then shot Wilson who was grappling with Bower, and Cummings who had grabbed a rifle. Gray swore that he had told his brother about the killing the evening of February 4, and that his brother had told Albert and Henry Jones. Jeff Gray told Buck Rice the next day, and Rice told J. P. Duncan. On the sixth, Gray told A. D. Norton, and on the seventh, Duncan. Thus, a number of cattlemen in the western part of the county knew about the crime immediately. All of these people were told, said Gray, because he feared that the sheepmen might come after him and he needed the protection these cattlemen could afford him. Somewhat later he told the Robinsons the same story. All of these people—plus several others—would soon come forth to report that Gray had indeed told them of the shooting long ago.

Needless to say, Diamondfield Jack and his attorneys were elated at the turn of events. This was the break they were waiting for. Now the pardon board would have a completely new set of evidence to consider, all of which dovetailed together smoothly in establishing Davis' innocence.

The Board of Pardons began its October, 1898, meeting by first considering all of the accumulated depositions and affidavits. A great deal of this material dealt with the original affidavits of Randolph Streeter and other Nevada residents who had heard Davis boast about a shooting scrape in Idaho. Much of it now seemed trivial, and Hawley was impatient to get on. At one point in the pardon board proceedings, according to the *Idaho Statesman,*

After the discussion had run on for some little time Mr. Hawley walked over near the wall, drew himself up to his full height and said somewhat dramatically: "Gentlemen, if any one can show that the threats or boasts that Davis at any time may have indulged in referred to the shooting of Cummings and Wilson, I will not ask you to hang Jack Davis, but I will be perfectly willing to take his place." And the attorney looked as though he meant it.[2]

Not only did the pardon board examine the various affidavits and documentary evidence, but it gathered opinions and appeals from interested citizens as well. By this time a number of petitions had been circulated in Cassia County seeking Davis' release on the basis of weaknesses in the original trial. Even before the Bower-Gray confession had influenced public opinion, many people already felt that justice had not been served in the way the trial had been handled. A typical petition is this one from Dry Creek:

To the Honorable Board of Pardons of the State of Idaho

Gentlemen:

We the undersigned citizens of Dry Creek, Cassia County, Idaho, respectfully petition your Honorable Board to grant a pardon to Jack Davis, who was convicted at the April, 1897, term of the District Court in and for Cassia County of the crime of murder in the first degree.

In support of our petition we urge among many reasons:

First, the evidence against Davis was entirely circumstantial.

Second, there is grave doubt as to his guilt.

Third, no portion of the evidence brought Davis nearer to the scene of the crime than about 20 miles, and then he was going in an opposite direction.

Fourth, Frank Smith, the principal witness for the prosecution was interested in securing a one-third portion of the reward of $4,800 offered for a conviction; that said Smith as a witness was unworthy of credit, admitting on the stand that he had assumed four different names in as many localities within a few years; that it would be a disgrace to the jurisprudence of the state to execute a person charged with crime upon the evidence of such a character as Frank Smith, when working for a reward.

Fifth, Fred Gleason, charged with assisting Davis in the perpetration of the same crime for which Davis was tried and convicted, and proven to have been the companion of Davis at the time the prosecution charges the crime to have been committed, was subsequently the same term of court tried and acquitted on substantially the same evidence upon which Davis was convicted.[3]

A list of signatures and occupations followed. The petition represented a good statement of Davis' position up until the confession by Bower and Gray. But the prosecution had not been idle while the defense had gathered signatures: Borah, too, was circulating petitions, urging the pardon board not to free Davis or commute his sentence.

The upshot of the October sessions of the pardon board was a reprieve for Diamondfield Jack until December 16, 1898, while the board could hold extended hearings on the new evidence. Early in December the board heard testimony from Bower, Gray, and the group of cattlemen to whom Gray had admitted the killing. Borah and Hawley examined the witnesses as did the members of the Board of Pardons—Governor Frank Steunenberg, Secretary of State George J. Lewis, and Attorney General R. E. McFarland. However, it was not what could be called an impartial board: Steunenberg was a sheepman, and McFarland, by virtue of his position, was the man with the overall responsibility of convicting Diamondfield Jack and making that conviction stick.

At the December hearing, for the first time, the charge was made that this was more than a murder case, that Diamondfield Jack was simply a pawn in some sort of behind-the-scenes struggle. Defense attorney Hawley made a long statement as an official witness before the board, noting that the inference had been made that the board was being deceived, that some sort of "deal" existed in the introduction of the Bower-Gray confession. He denied that any such scheme existed within the defense staff, and invited the board members to inspect all of his office correspondence since the day he entered the case in the employ of John Sparks.

At this point an interesting three-way exchange took place among James Hawley, Governor Frank Steunenberg, and William E. Borah.

Hawley: My reasons for making this statement are these: In the first place, extraordinary as these circumstances are, I feel that some explanation is due from counsel who have participated in this matter and who have had control of it, because it is probably the most extraordinary combination of circumstances that ever occurred in the Northwest in a trial of any kind; and I feel, under the circumstances, that it is incumbent upon me to make a statement of this kind. I understand that there is a doubt, either from the evidence itself or from the statements of others, or in the minds of the gentlemen representing the Sheep Growers' or Wool Growers' Association, or their attorneys, about the bona fideness of this matter; that it has been urged or at least argued that instead of this application being made in good faith, that it is an attempt to hoodwink and deceive this Board; that persons, in order to save the life of another, have seen fit to perjure themselves in regard to this affair, and I desire to say and again pledge my honor both as a man and as an attorney, that I cannot, in the light of correspondence I have had and the efforts that I have made, culminating in this matter, imagine for one moment, that I have been deceived. . . .

Steunenberg: . . . If the feelings you attribute to this board are true, so far as I know, they have never been mentioned in any regular meeting of this Board, or in any conference or consultation.

Hawley: . . . I do not desire to make anything in the nature of a charge. If my position is not correct, I have either been seeking to hoodwink this Board and the public, or I have been deceived myself . . . I have either been a knave or a fool.

Borah: I will say to the Board and counsel in this case, that as far as the prosecution is concerned, it has never for a moment supposed that Mr. Hawley or Mr. Perky, either one, has been either a knave or a fool. We had believed and still believe that they have been misled themselves as to certain statements. It is evident that there has been lying done in this case, and lots of it; but we would not intimate that Mr. Hawley or Mr. Perky—

Steunenberg: While I appreciate the position you take in this, I do not see what could be gained, looking at it from a practical point of view, by pursuing any investigation along the lines you suggest. If we were to take it up, it might create an impression in your mind and in the minds of the public that we did believe that counsel had been in collusion. As far as I know this Board has never entertained such an idea. . . .

Hawley: . . . This is what I wish to say, and the correspondence would show it, should there exist in the minds of the Board the idea that a play is being made, I not only want this Board to be satisfied, I want the parties interested to be satisfied, I want the world to be satisfied.

Borah: The prosecution in this case is satisfied as far as your statement is concerned.

Steunenberg: I am inclined to believe at the present time that this is an unprofitable discussion.

Hawley: I make it as a tender.

Borah: We have believed that there is collusion in this matter, but no one supposed that Mr. Hawley or Mr. Perky was the father of it.[4]

The transcript of Hawley's appearance before the board ends at this point, and there is no further reference to collusion in the transcript of the rest of the December hearing. However, it is clear from the vigorous cross-examination employed by Borah against witnesses who supported the Bower-Gray story that the prosecutor still felt that there was an organized effort to cover up certain facts.

At least six such witnesses confirmed the Bower-Gray confession. The stories of the two men not only confirmed each other, but they explained some of the weaknesses and discrepancies of the original prosecution case. The corncob pipe—up to this point completely unexplained—indicated that Bower could have been at the scene of the murder. Other evidence such as powder burns, the location of the slugs, the position of the bodies—all could be explained better by the Bower-Gray story than by the prosecution's version of the shooting. Only a few discrepancies remained. Both Gray and Bower said that they saw or heard no dogs around the wagon. This might be explained by the dogs having been asleep when the two men arrived, but seemingly the gunfire would have awakened them. Another discrepancy remained with Davis Hunter's identification of the man on the road; he now insisted in an affidavit presented to the board that the man he met with Bower was definitely not Jeff Gray.

The board was now in a position in which they had to seek additional testimony in order not to offend public opinion. So they voted two-to-one to grant another reprieve to Diamondfield Jack until February 1, 1899. Attorney General R. E. McFarland dissented on this vote; he said:

I disagree with the majority of the Board of Pardons in the adoption of the resolution continuing the above entitled case and extending the reprieve of Jack Davis for the following reasons:

1. The case has already been postponed twice and no good or sufficient reason exists for a further continuance.

2. The attorneys representing both petitioner and the prosecution have informed the Board that all the facts and circumstances in connection with the case and within their knowledge and control have been presented to the Board, and there is no hope or prospect of any further light being thrown upon the horrible occurrence which has resulted in petitioner's conviction for the crime of murder.

3. The Board during its investigation and deliberation of petitioner's application has had before it a transcript of all the evidence and proceedings upon which conviction was had, and upon which the Supreme Court passed in affirming the judgment, besides the oral testimony of numerous witnesses, and affidavits and counter affidavits filed by the respective parties to the proceedings which certainly ought to be sufficient to justify a decision one way or another.

4. The expenses of the trial, and the cost and expenses of maintaining and keeping the prisoner throughout the trial and proceedings in this case which have covered more than two years, have been sufficiently onerous upon Cassia County, and I do not feel disposed to inflict any further burden upon it in this behalf.

5. I do not believe it right or just for the retiring members of this Board to avoid the responsibility of an unpleasant duty by bequeathing it to their successors.[5]

The final sentence in this statement was a reference to the fact that by this time both the attorney general and the secretary of state were lame-duck officials, voted out of office the previous month. Steunenberg had been reelected governor on the combined Democrat–Silver Republican ticket, but McFarland and Lewis represented the old-line Democratic and the Populist-Democratic tradition, respectively, so they were not renominated in the Free Silver wave of 1898.

Idaho's political situation in the 1890's was one of confusion and rapid change. Populism and free-silver appeared as successive waves of public opinion. Candidates changed parties regularly without offending voters, because the voters were changing just as rapidly. Even William E. Borah, generally regarded as a rock-ribbed Republican, had run for Congress in 1896 on the same coalition silver ticket as Frank Steunenberg, one of the strongest Democrats in the state. But toward the end of the 1890's, although silver still served as a political bond, voters were getting more selective and voting split tickets. Thus, from beginning to end, the Diamondfield Jack case extended through the tenure of five different pardon boards—a situation which did not help Davis' chances of a pardon.

The January, 1899, meeting of the board was held in Albion to allow Diamondfield Jack to testify before the board. Rather than conducting a question and answer examination of Davis, Governor Steunenberg invited the prisoner to make an oral statement. In a long rambling speech the garrulous gunman covered many aspects of the case, but he probably did his cause little or no good because of the hostility he expressed toward everyone. Oliver Dunn, the sheepman, had poisoned his grub out on the range, he said; that was why he felt strongly about his personal feud with the sheepmen. The Tolman shooting was self-defense; he had planned to give himself up afterwards but he was afraid of the treatment he would get in Albion. "I believed the Mormons would lynch me, and I got up and pulled out." He kept the religious issue alive later in the testimony when he asserted, "The Mormon church is against me, and was after me all the way through."

No one was spared Diamondfield Jack's wrath during the hearing, except possibly his benefactor—cattle baron John Sparks. Davis told the board that his lawyers had deserted him—that at key moments during the last two years Perky had visited him when Hawley should have come, and vice versa. The prosecution was out to hang him, come hell or high water, he insisted. He flatly accused Borah of bribing the witnesses from Nevada who had testified to his boasting there.

It was probably this last charge and others like it that alienated the board against the prisoner more than anything else. The testimony and affidavits showed that Davis had done a lot of boasting in Nevada about a shooting scrape with sheepherders in Idaho, but there was only one unverified statement saying that Davis had claimed to have killed the men on Deep Creek— and that one could be discounted if you remembered that Davis was not only drunk at the time but that he was known to be a chronic boaster and liar. If Davis had admitted to the board that he was given to boasting and that he possibly created the impression in Nevada that he was involved in the Deep Creek affair, the board might have been much more favorably inclined. But, instead, he was belligerent.

In other ways, too, Davis hurt his own cause. He

now claimed that he was alone at the Dunn camp the night of the shooting there; by denying the previous version of the story he was cutting himself off from being with Fred Gleason who had already been acquitted. He also denied that Bower told him at Wells on the sixth about the killing; by doing this Davis seems to have been more interested in refuting the testimony of Dayley, the deputized sheepman who helped bring him back, than in supporting a plausible explanation of the shooting. So, regardless of whether Diamondfield Jack told the truth or lied on various aspects of the case, his vindictiveness before the board must have hurt his chances.

In only a few places did the other side of Jack Davis emerge, revealing him as a weak and helpless man caught up in a strange and complex web of circumstances. In explaining his behavior in Nevada he denied that he was a heavy drinker of hard liquor, but he did admit that he was a great consumer of port wine. And he offered a candid alibi for not making the alleged murder ride; he said that during his sojourn in Wells in January, 1896, he had acquired one of the occupational diseases of off-duty cowboys: gonorrhea. His venereal disease, he claimed, would have made such a ride extremely uncomfortable, if not impossible.

The pardon board again heard testimony for the Cassia County cattlemen Alex Gray, A. D. Norton, J. P. Duncan, and Buck Rice which confirmed the Jeff Gray and J. E. Bower confessions. In addition, John Sparks testified that his superintendent, Bower, had overtaken him in Ogden immediately after the shooting, and told him the full story of self-defense. But the board did not seem interested in or impressed by the new evidence. On January 23, 1899, they denied the pardon application of Diamondfield Jack Davis, and resentenced him to hang on February 1.

Up to now, the question of whether or not Davis would hang had been, for the most part, an academic one. Now it became a very real one. In Albion construction began on the gallows. Hawley now turned to the federal courts for the first time. On the twenty-eighth of January the United States District Court in Boise denied an application for a *habeas corpus* writ. Hawley quickly sent an appeal to the U.S. Circuit Court of Appeals, Ninth Judicial District, in San Francisco. Judge Beatty of this court, an ex-Idahoan who had presided over the 1892 Couer d'Alene labor trials, replied on the thirtieth with an order staying the execution while the appeal was pending.

The stay was received in Boise the day before Diamondfield Jack was due to die in Albion, 175 miles away. Getting word of this action to the sheriff now became a major problem. There was no telegraph line into the Cassia County seat, and only an unpredictable telephone line which was often out of order. Hawley feared that the telephone line might be tampered with by the over-zealous sheepmen, so he dispatched his young law partner Will Puckett on the afternoon eastbound train with three copies of the reprieve. Arrangements were quickly made for two other riders to meet Puckett in Minidoka, the closest station on the Oregon Short Line, some twenty-five miles north of Albion.

Each of the three men was to take a copy of the stay of execution to the sheriff in Albion, riding alone and by different routes. Hawley obviously figured that the sheepmen would try to intercept the document.

The people of Albion had gone to bed that evening anticipating that they would witness the hanging of Diamondfield Jack the following day. Davis had watched the testing of the gallows in the jailyard, and had pronounced the structure capable of doing the job. During the last few days he had been relaxed and talkative; he ate and slept well. He had whiled away the time making hair ropes and trinkets for some children who visited the jail. He seemed confident either that dying was no great problem, or else that he would not die at all. He gave a final statement to Charles Mark, the courageous editor of the Albion *Times* who had befriended him. The statement was to be made public after the execution.

Through the winter chill of January 31, three horsemen galloped toward Albion. Late at night the first of the three riders arrived at the county seat. It was Will Puckett. He had encountered no trouble from sheepmen along the dark ride, and neither had the two other men who arrived shortly afterwards. The sheriff, O. P. Anderson, was roused out of bed. He was happy to see the legal papers stopping the execution. He had already told the pardon board that he thought Davis was innocent, and besides, he had gotten to like the cantankerous cowboy in his charge. And so Albion was denied its execution. Diamondfield Jack's case was now in a federal court, and he had discovered that he still had a few friends in this world.

NOTES

[1]Bower's deposition is taken verbatim from the original in the Hawley papers. Records of the pardon board contain depositions setting forth the other facts of this chapter.

[2]*Idaho Statesman,* October 19, 1898.

[3]This petition is representative of several preserved in the Hawley papers.

[4]Transcript of the Board of Pardons hearing for December 2, 1898, found in the Hawley papers.

[5]From McFarland's dissent, December 6, 1898, preserved in the Hawley papers.

Diamondfield Jack in his affluent years in Nevada. (From the *Tonopah Sun,* 1905, drawn by Arthur V. Buel. Courtesy of Nevada Historical Society)

John Sparks (right) later became governor of Nevada. He is shown here in casual garb with J. W. Dorsey, his attorney. (Courtesy of Nevada Historical Society)

6

The End of the Legal Trail

LIFE IN ALBION returned to normal. Charles Mark, the newspaper editor, opened the final statement which Jack Davis had given to him and found nothing incriminating in it—nothing other than the same avowal of innocence which Davis had consistently offered.

Now that Diamondfield Jack had been given what appeared to be a lengthy reprieve, Cassia County would have to act on the Bower-Gray confession. Routine legal procedures had already begun; in the fall of 1898 a warrant had been sworn by Fred Wilson, a sheepman, for the arrest of Bower and Gray. Bower had his preliminary hearing in October at which $10,000 bond was provided by A. D. Norton and John Sparks. Gray was arraigned in Albion in November before probate judge S. P. Weatherman; his bail, also $10,000, was posted by a group of cattlemen including the Jones brothers, Louis Soloman, and A. Burstrom.

At Gray's hearing, Bower repeated the details of his confession and what he had already deposed to the pardon board. Bower's admission was borne out by Rice, Harris, Robinson, and Norton. The stories fit together smoothly, generally showing that Bower and Gray were present at the shooting. Even before the pardon board had expressed its opinion on the matter, Gray was bound over to district court. B. P. Howells, the new county attorney who had succeeded John Rogers, was not happy with the prospect of prosecuting Gray. In January he moved to dismiss the charges on the grounds that there was no chance of conviction. But Judge Stockslager denied the motion, and the trial was set for Jeff Gray on February 16, 1899, in Albion.

Jeff Gray was a likable and high-spirited young man with many friends and relatives in the area. He was the son of a onetime Montana Indian fighter who had turned squawman by marrying a half-breed Indian. The Grays were small cattlemen in Cassia County. The boys, Jeff, Andrew, and Alex, hired out to other cattlemen while the daughter married Henry, one of the Jones brothers. Since Jeff Gray had once worked on Sparks-Harrell ranches, John Sparks assumed the cost of his defense.

Sparks, of course, also provided for Bower's defense. In an interesting sidelight to this pretrial interlude, Bower decided that he wanted erstwhile prosecutor William E. Borah as his defense attorney. Hawley agreed that it would be worth trying; in a letter to John Sparks he said, "I would rather have Borah's assistance in either or both of these cases than any other man I know of." But there was an obvious conflict of interest to Borah, and he stayed out of the case completely.

This left Jim Hawley as the chief defense attorney, assisted by W. L. McGuinness and by the regular Sparks-Harrell counsel, J. W. Dorsey, a man who was later to become very active in various aspects of the legal fight in the courts and with the pardon board.

B. P. Howells reluctantly prosecuted Gray. At the trial Bower and Gray both told their stories, along with the various cattlemen who had consistently confirmed their stories in previous hearings and depositions. The case against Gray was weak as a first-degree murder prosecution. Judge Stockslager clinched the case when he instructed the jury on the question of self-defense:

> If the jury believe from the evidence that James E. Bower and the defendant were in company, and while they were together as companions, said Bower was assaulted by the deceased in such a way as to induce in the defendant a reasonable and well-founded belief either that he was actually in danger, or that said James E. Bower was actually in danger, of losing his life or of suffering great bodily harm, then the defendant was justified in defending himself, or defending said James E. Bower, whether the danger was real or only apparent.[1]

With this kind of instruction the jury's decision was almost prescribed for them. On February 21, 1899, after brief deliberations they returned a *not guilty* verdict on Gray. Two days later Hawley had obtained the signatures of eleven of the twelve jurors on an affidavit describing how they had arrived at their verdict. They swore,

> . . . that we did believe from the evidence that he was there at said killing and did kill those men, as stated in his

evidence and the evidence of James E. Bower, and that he was acquitted, as far as our votes were concerned, upon the ground and for the reason that it was shown by said testimony that the shots fired by the said Gray were fired by him in defense of J. E. Bower and himself. That the evidence taken as a whole, in our judgments, showed that Gray was justifiable [*sic*] in shooting, and it was upon this ground that we voted for his acquittal.[2]

Hawley had carried out an effective maneuver. Gray had been acquitted, but the jury had deposed that it was because he killed Wilson in self defense. From the standpoint of legal strategy the only thing that might have been better was the conviction of Gray: no appeals court could have refused to free Davis if another man had been properly convicted of the same crime. But this was the next best thing: a sworn statement by the jurors saying that Gray killed Wilson, but was innocent of murder because he did it in self-defense.

In the fall of 1899 Cassia County went through the motions of trying Bower, but it was a lost cause from the very beginning. Sparks-Harrell attorneys again took over the defense. In a short trial Bower was acquitted of the charge of killing Wilson, and the charges against him in connection with Cummings' death were dropped.

In the meantime an interesting series of legal events was taking place which would further complicate the situation. Shortly after Diamondfield Jack's reprieve from the gallows in January of 1899 the Idaho legislature passed a law which required that all executions be carried out at the state penitentiary in Boise. Since he was still a "death row" prisoner Davis was moved from the jail in Albion to the prison. But the Cassia County sheriff, through prosecutor William E. Borah, sued in the state Supreme Court for a *habeas corpus* writ to regain custody of the prisoner. This move was apparently designed to prevent defense attorney Hawley from stopping any future execution on the grounds that the 1899 legislation had changed the punishment for murder, and thus was unconstitutional in Davis' case as an *ex post facto* law. Borah's suspicions proved correct, for Hawley as *amicus curiae* (friend of the court) not only contended that the statute was unconstitutional, but that it repealed the existing murder statute. Thus, *no* statute existed under which Davis could be hanged.

The Idaho Supreme Court late in December of 1899 ruled that the change in execution site was indeed an *ex post facto* law with respect to previously sentenced prisoners. Therefore, the court decreed, Davis should rightfully be executed at the Cassia County jail under the old law, instead of at the penitentiary under the new statute. It looked as though Borah had outmaneuvered Hawley on this point. As a result, Diamondfield Jack spent a gloomy Christmas back in his Albion jail cell, knowing that he was once again eligible for a Cassia County hanging.[3]

The whole *amicus curiae* episode was, of course, a diversionary feint on the part of Hawley. He was certainly too wise in the ways of courts to expect that Davis would be freed as a result of this strategy. But it consumed several months of litigation, and every month was important now while other legal appeals were still pending.

Hawley's primary legal efforts for Davis were now directed toward the appeals courts. From 1891 until 1911 there existed in the United States two separate sets of federal appellate courts, the U.S. Circuit Court and the U.S. Circuit Court of Appeals.[4] It was a confusing arrangement. Using largely the same personnel, the two courts had jurisdiction over somewhat different cases and procedures. The Circuit Court of Appeals, which handled appeals from District Courts, had saved Davis' life in January of 1899 with the stay of execution after the District Court had refused a *habeas corpus* writ. In October of 1899 this court affirmed the District Court by denying the writ on the grounds of want of jurisdiction, since a construction of the federal constitution—the *ex post facto* law—was involved. In other words, Hawley had chosen the wrong route; such questions belonged in the U.S. Supreme Court, and could get there only through the Circuit Courts.[5] But Hawley had succeeded in buying nine more months of life for Davis through the erroneous appeal, so it may have been a deliberate strategy on his part.

He then turned to the other court, the U.S. Circuit Court for the State of Idaho, with another application for a *habeas corpus* writ. This time he presented two arguments. First he argued ingeniously that the original conviction of Davis was illegal since it grew out of a prosecution by information. Such prosecutions were unconstitutional in Idaho, said Hawley, inasmuch as the 1891 legislature which wrote the law made certain procedural errors in passing the legislation. Second, he continued arguing that the *ex post facto* features of the change in execution site rendered the entire law illegal. The Circuit Court denied the writ, but left the door open for an appeal to the U.S. Supreme Court. Early in 1900 the case was accepted by the high court and placed on its fall docket.

In the meantime something else was happening which, although completely unrelated to the Diamond-field Jack affair, conceivably could affect the fate of Davis. In the spring of 1899 violent labor troubles erupted in the Coeur d'Alene mining country of northern Idaho. Property was dynamited and several men were killed. Governor Steunenberg asked for and received federal troops to control the situation, inasmuch as all of Idaho's militiamen were then in the Philippines for the Spanish-American War.

When law and order were restored in the summer of 1899 Hawley and Borah joined together as special prosecutors for the state in the trial of a number of miners arrested during the labor troubles. Idaho often made use of special "high-powered" prosecutors in such cases, as witnessed by Borah's and Powers' participation in the Diamondfield Jack case. Now Borah and Hawley were put together to form what Idahoans generally acknowledged was the greatest legal team in the state—and perhaps the West.

The "test case" of the Coeur d'Alene troubles was that of a young union leader, Paul Corcoran. With vigorous and imaginative prosecution by the two special attorneys, Corcoran was convicted of killing an employee of a mining company, and sentenced to life imprisonment. This case, and the others related to it, occupied both Hawley and Borah through 1899 and part of 1900. If the state had been free to hang Diamondfield Jack during this busy period Hawley might have had great difficulty preventing it, since he was so completely tied up with the Coeur d'Alene cases. But, thanks to Hawley's strategy, Davis was alive and safe during this period as the Idaho Supreme Court, the U.S. Circuit Courts, and the U.S. Supreme Court considered his case.

In December of 1900 the United States Supreme Court heard Davis' case and announced its verdict. It was another dreary Christmas present for Hawley and his client. The court affirmed the Circuit Court decision and refused to issue the writ.[6] To Hawley's first point about prosecutions by information it answered: since the point had not been argued in two previous appearances before the Idaho Supreme Court, the federal courts could not issue a writ based on a person's being deprived of liberty until the state court appeal had been denied. On the *ex post facto* question the Supreme Court decision agreed with the lower courts that changing the punishment for an offense does not have the effect of freeing all of the prisoners who were convicted when the punishment was something else.

So Diamondfield Jack's appeals to the federal courts came to an end; there was no longer any further recourse in law. But the wheels of justice move slowly; Hawley's efforts had added a total of twenty-three months to the life of Jack Davis. And during those twenty-three months much had been happening.

After the beginning of 1899 the letters that poured into the Idaho pardon board were almost completely pro-Davis. Charles Mark of the Albion *Times* called this change in public opinion to the attention of the board; he noted that now his editorials favoring release of Davis were well received in the community where once they had precipitated boycotts and sanctions against the paper. In other letters to the board, Hardy Sears, who had been county commissioner at the time of the Diamondfield Jack trial, agreed that public opinion had greatly changed since the trial; Edwin M. Holden expressed a similar view.

Several letter writers commented on the injustice of the whole affair. S. P. Weatherman, the probate judge who had handled several of the preliminary hearings, said that Davis was wrongfully convicted, and described his pending execution rather quaintly as "equivalent to almost, if not quite, murder." O. R. Hale, an attorney, also protested that the "hanging of Jack Davis would be judicial murder."

Some interesting things were said in these letters about the prejudice—political and religious—which existed in the area at the time of the trial and several years thereafter. Editor Mark of the Albion *Times* said:

My honest opinion about the matter is that it is nothing more than a political fight pure and simple. The Republicans have brought the matter into every campaign since 1896, and not one man who ever signed a petition favorable to Jack Davis can get a vote out of Oakley. Indeed, you have no idea of the conditions existing in this county politically, and the only way to become acquainted with them is to reside here.[7]

A similar reference was made by Frank Redke who, in reporting to the board that Gray had once admitted the shooting to him, spoke of Oakley as "the hot bed of Mark Hanna." It is interesting to note that Cassia County, along with the rest of Idaho, had gone Populist and Democrat–Silver Republican in the unsettled 1890's, but by 1900 was once again staunchly Republican. Even C. A. Stockslager, who had presided over the Diamondfield Jack trial, failed to carry Cassia County when he ran successfully on the Democratic ticket for the state Supreme Court in 1900. In this connection it is worth noting that increasingly in Idaho in the next few years the Republicans became the "law and order" party. As Stockslager found out in Cassia County in 1900 (and throughout the state six years later when he failed in a try for the governorship), it was not enough to be a stern "law and order" man if you happened to be a Democrat.

Religious prejudice in Cassia County also came in for its share of criticism to the board. W. D. Fuller, who had been a juror in the Gleason case, wrote the board to say,

The jury that tried Davis was composed largely of Mormons. I do not want to attack any body's religion but the men killed were Mormons, and they believe in blood atonement. The foreman of the jury and two others of the jury told me after the trial that "If Davis wasn't guilty he had done enough and ought to be hanged on general principles."

The County Attorney's wife (Mrs. Howells) said in my house that they wouldn't prosecute Bower and Gray for the killing because if they did Davis would get away from them.[8]

Similar sentiments were expressed in a long letter written by a man who signed his name in an impressive flowing hand as W. S. St. Cyr. Said he,

When you find a community that depends entirely on its church for justice you will find little of it weighed out in court, and that especially when the man being tried is unfortunate enough to not be a member of that church. I allude to the Mormon church and the Mormon faith.[9]

St. Cyr went on to talk about Mormon public officials exerting pressure on people in the community, particularly in getting them to withdraw signatures on petitions. It was true that after each group of petitions had been received by the pardon board there were generally a few letters asking that names be withdrawn.

Another line of argument advanced by those who sought Davis' freedom dealt with the character of the prisoner. A number of people pointed out that he did not appear to be the hired-killer type originally depicted by the prosecution. Mrs. George E. Bowen, wife of a jailer who had guarded Davis, assured the board that Davis was a "jentilman in evrie respect." M. T. Brown, a sheriff who had guarded him at the prison, reported that he had never heard Davis make an incriminating remark. Davis, according to Brown, was "not destitute of refinement," and was fond of women, children, horses, pets, and even flowers, which he grew in his cell. W. W. Adamson, another deputy who had guarded him, described Davis as an ideal prisoner; so did O. P. Anderson, onetime sheriff of Cassia County.

Only a few voices were raised in defense of the original conviction. One was that of H. R. Cahoon, foreman of the Diamondfield Jack jury, who insisted to the very end that the jury verdict was correct. Another was that of William E. Borah, who, although now out of the case, continued to assure the pardon board that some kind of "deal" had been made by the defense in the Bower-Gray confession. The only lengthy petition which was submitted to the pardon board opposing the release of Davis was signed by a number of relatives of jurors intimately involved in the case. For example, juror Cahoon and one of his relatives signed; juror Durfee and five relatives signed; and juror Wake from the hamlet of Ward signed, along with three other Wakes and four Wards. So the organized opposition to Davis' release came from tiny pockets of Cassia County sheepmen, or from jurors who perhaps feared retaliation if Davis were turned loose.

But there remained an enormous amount of organized resistance elsewhere. The *Idaho Statesman* of Boise, the leading newspaper of the state, was adamantly opposed to Diamondfield Jack to the bitter end. The other Boise paper, the *Evening Capital News,* vigorously criticized the vindictive attitude of the *Statesman,* referring to the rival paper as the "paid attorney of a powerful interest" and as the "morning mummy." Political charges did not figure too prominently in this newspaper battle, however. This was because the *Capital News* as a Democratic paper could not get too partisan in its attacks on the Republicanism of the *Statesman* and the Cassia County sheepmen since the third group of militant "Davis-must-die" advocates were the top men of the Democratic state administration.

Elected to office in 1900 were three new members of the pardon board. Frank Steunenberg had not chosen to seek reelection as governor; he was succeeded by another Democrat, Frank Hunt. Two candidates of the still-powerful Democratic–Silver Republican fusion ticket won the other two key statehouse posts: C. J. Bassett replaced Mark Patrie as Secretary of State, and Frank Martin succeeded S. H. Hays as Attorney General. These men constituted the third separate pardon board to deal directly with the case of Davis. Whether they would be more open-minded than the other two remained to be seen.

But before this pardon board ever considered the Diamondfield Jack affair, James Hawley tried one last legal maneuver. In April of 1901 he moved for a new trial in the district court of Cassia County on the grounds of newly-discovered evidence, specifically the test rides of 1897 which showed the near-impossibility of the alleged murder ride. Hawley argued that the normal diligence of the defense at the time of the first trial could not have turned up this evidence, since the defense lawyers did not know that the state was going to claim that the ride and the murder were carried out in half a day's time. But Judge Stewart denied the motion, pointing out that the law required that such appeals be made within ten days of the original conviction. Stewart—who once had been Borah's law partner—then went on to resentence Diamondfield Jack to hang on June 21, 1901.

The Idaho statute under which Judge Stewart made his ruling specified: "Application for a new trial . . . must be made within ten days after verdict, unless the court or judge extends the time." Hawley then turned to the Idaho Supreme Court, which now included Stockslager, the sheepman, for a "Certificate of Probable Cause" for such extension, but the high court on June 17, 1901—just four days before the scheduled hanging—refused to intervene.[10]

During this time, however, the pardon board indicated that they were willing to review the whole affair. They inspected the enormous amount of correspondence and depositions, and scheduled a meeting for the end of June. Judge Stewart and the board apparently agreed to change the execution date. July 3, 1901, then became the next date set, toward which the gallows and other preparations in Albion were actually made.

Many of the letters and statements examined by the board in June have already been mentioned here. Several other key communications need to be considered at this point. Davis himself wrote a ninety-three-page letter in longhand to the governor. It was an interesting document, throwing considerable light on the man's personality and on his surprisingly bourgeois code of morals. The punctuation and capitalization of the letter were weak, but the style, the grammar, and the spelling were all good. There was nothing new or startling in the message, however; instead Davis repeated his old attacks and accusations. He did include one new target—Judge Stewart. The judge was prejudiced against him, he said, because the judge was a sheep man. While this may have been the case, Davis seems to have ignored a more provable kind of prejudice: the fact that Stewart had once been William Borah's law partner.

Perhaps the most important messages to the pardon board came from two of the men who had originally prosecuted Diamondfield Jack—John C. Rogers of Cassia County and O. W. Powers of Salt Lake City. Both men now believed Davis innocent. Rogers stated that he was not originally convinced by the Bower-Gray confession, but the solidness of all aspects of proof since that time had ultimately convinced him.

> My conviction has grown with my investigations that the case of the state against Jack Davis will have to go down with a long line of similar cases found in the books where strong combinations of circumstances have led a honest jury to a false conclusion—the conviction of a man innocent of the crime charged against him.[11]

Rogers also placed his name first on a petition for a full pardon which was signed by a number of prominent Idaho people.

Orlando W. Powers was equally candid. Concerning Davis, he had this to say to the Board of Pardons:

> He was convicted upon circumstantial evidence, and the confession of Bower and Gray, if it had been produced at the trial of Davis, would have made conviction impossible in my opinion. I prosecuted Davis with all the vigor I could,

as I believed him guilty beyond a reasonable doubt. The case now is changed by the subsequent developments and if he shall be executed there is a question whether or not a man not connected with the crime has suffered.[12]

Powers went on to explain why he now believed Davis innocent. He also recalled that the introduction of the corncob pipe at the original trial had caused "manifest nervousness" to Bower in the courtroom, and that he, Powers, had commented on this to one of the other prosecutors at the time. However, he did not believe the story of the struggle in self-defense; said Powers:

Deponent does not propose to pass upon the credibility of Bower or of Gray. If deponent did so he would state as his belief that no such struggle took place as they state. But, the fact remains to confront all who choose to investigate this matter, that it is scarcely probable that the jury would have convicted Davis, if the testimony of Bower and Gray had been produced. For it seems incredible that two men, in order to save the life of a man apparently as worthless as Jack Davis, would confess to the taking of human lives.[13]

Kirtland I. Perky, one of the original defense lawyers and now a district judge, deposed along similar lines. He, too, had noticed that Bower seemed ill at ease during the trial of Davis. He also reported that Fred Gleason had once told him of meeting a man in Nevada who remembered Bower saying on February 5, 1896, that "there were two dead men up on Shoshone Basin." Perky also explained that Bower had been concerned about Jeff Gray's drinking; the lawyer had an understanding with Bower to provide whatever legal assistance Gray might need as a result of his drunken tongue.

Under the pressure of all the opinions expressed by these letter writers, many of whom were influential citizens, the pardon board was finally forced to move. Actually after six months in office Governor Hunt, Secretary of State Bassett, and Attorney General Martin had not yet had their first formal meeting as the Board of Pardons in the case of Jack Davis. But their review of the correspondence directed to them in recent months showed clearly that public opinion had indeed swung around squarely behind the cowboy. A public hearing definitely seemed necessary. However, while the board was still discussing the case, Davis' newest execution date had arrived. It was July 3, 1901; something had to be done.

The easiest way out was the temporary expedient of granting another short stay while the board held a formal hearing. So, for the eighth time, Davis was given a respite, this one extending the execution date to the seventeenth of July. But by waiting until the actual day of the hanging, July 3, to grant the extension the board was acting recklessly. What was happening meantime at Albion where the sheriff had the discretion of carrying out the sentence at any hour of his choice on July 3? The *Capital News* reported on the afternoon of the third:

> The action of the board today was wired to the Sheriff at Albion. The message goes by wire, however, only to Minidoka, the nearest station on the Short Line road. From there it is telephoned to the sheriff. As the hanging of Davis

was to have taken place today at the court house in Albion, unless the respite was received, there is of course much responsibility in getting the message through safely. In order to insure the delivery of the information, the attorneys have arranged with the sheriff to have two cow-boys at the depot at Minidoka with orders for 2 copies of the telegram. These they will secure and then ride with the messages as fast as relays of horses will carry them to Albion, a distance of 28 miles. They will have two relays of horses. So that in the event the telephone wire is tampered with, the sheriff will still be sure of getting the information.[14]

It was 1899 all over again! Hawley had anticipated the inept handling of the stay of execution by the board, and had lined up two riders to get the telegram into the hands of the Cassia County sheriff as soon as possible. The telegram was sent from Boise at 10:05 A.M. Waiting in Minidoka were two young cowboys, Willis Sears and Charley Krise. Riding hard, in single file for protection against any possible ambush, the two men raced their horses across the lava beds to Marsh Lake where fresh horses were waiting. The second pair of mounts took them to Vulcan Ferry on the Snake River where they changed again for the final dash south through the hills to Albion.

When they reached the Cassia County seat they found that they were in time. Sheriff Adams had not planned on carrying out the execution for another three hours yet if no word came—and word *had* come. Just as Sheriff Anderson had been happy to forego hanging Diamondfield Jack in 1899, Sheriff Adams was relieved to know that Davis had been spared again. He, too, as Anderson before him, had become rather fond of the garrulous gunman who had spent so long in the Cassia County jail.

Albion missed its execution once more. The gallows had been readied, the hangman hired, and a crowd had again gathered to see the execution—all for naught. But this time there seemed to be a genuine sense of relief, not disappointment, when the execution was called off. Cassia County had come to its senses.

NOTES

[1]The instructions in the Gray trial are preserved in the Hawley papers.

[2]Hawley's affidavit, signed by the jurors, is preserved in the Hawley papers.

[3]The controversy over the site of executions is described in Mac-Lane, *A Sagebrush Lawyer*.

[4]The explanation of the dual appeals court is in Roscoe Pound, *Organization of Courts*.

[5]The denial of the writ on the grounds of want of jurisdiction is reported in *Davis* v. *Burke,* 38 CCA 299, and in *Davis* v. *Burke,* 97 Fed. Rep. 501.

[6]The decisions of the United States Circuit Court and the United States Supreme Court are in *Davis* v. *Burke,* 179 US 399.

[7]Letter from Charles S. Mark to Governor Frank W. Hunt, June 29, 1901, preserved in the Hawley papers.

[8]Letter from W. D. Fuller to the Board of Pardons, June 29, 1901, preserved in the Hawley papers.

[9]Letter from W. S. St. Cyr to the Board of Pardons, July 1, 1901, preserved in the Hawley papers.

[10]The decision denying the motion for a new trial is in *State* v. *Davis,* 8 Idaho 115. The statute was number 7953, Revised Idaho Statutes.

[11]Letter from John C. Rogers to the Board of Pardons, July 8, 1901, preserved in the Hawley papers.

[12]Deposition by O. W. Powers to the Board of Pardons, June 24, 1901, preserved in the Hawley papers.

[13]*Ibid.*

[14]*Evening Capital News,* July 3, 1901.

Diamondfield Jack, with his notorious background, was a colorful addition to parades in the Nevada boomtowns. He is shown here (front right) in the 1905 Memorial Day parade in Goldfield. (Courtesy of Frank P. Tondel)

7

Twilight for the Gods of Vengeance

WITH A REPRIEVE of only two weeks granted to Diamondfield Jack, the Idaho Board of Pardons found itself faced with the responsibility of decisive and prompt action. Governor Hunt, Secretary of State Bassett, and Attorney General Martin met officially in Boise as the board, and continued their review of the mountain of documentary evidence confronting them. For the most part James Hawley did not present anything new to the board, but merely pointed out the various key depositions and testimony previously presented in support of the Bower-Gray version of the shooting.

In summing up the results of this hearing J. W. Dorsey, the Sparks-Harrell attorney, made a rather eloquent plea to the board which prompted the *Statesman* to comment:

He [Dorsey] said it had remained for the state of Idaho to produce the most tangled, strange, anomalous case in history. It was a pathetic tragedy, which could do credit to the marvelous genius of a Bret Harte, a Conan Doyle, or an Old Sleuth. Mr. Dorsey put into his opening all the short paragraphs, impressive periods, and red-letter expressions customary to the yellow-back novel writers. With a thumb in each pantaloons pocket he stood before the board and a number of visitors and made an opening that caused a thrill of enthusiasm to pass through each auditor, and gave them firm belief in his histrionic ability.[1]

Hawley was equally effective in capturing the interest of the board and the curious spectators. The *Capital News,* always a strong political backer of Hawley, had this to say:

At this time Hon. James H. Hawley commenced his argument, and for two and one half hours he talked as only an able and eloquent attorney can when his client is in the shadow of the gallows, and when the outcome depends very much upon the way the various phases of the case are presented. The attorney made as eloquent a plea as was ever heard in Idaho, and whatever the outcome it was understood that all the argument and pleading possible was presented by the attorney in summing up the case.[2]

To what degree the board members were influenced, either by this kind of forensic rhetoric or by the pressures of public opinion, it is impossible to determine. But their ultimate reaction came as a surprise, an even greater break in the case than the Bower-Gray confession had been some three years earlier. But it was a strange and indefensible action.

On July 16, 1901, one day before Davis was again slated to hang, the pardon board commuted his sentence to life imprisonment! The explanation made by the board to the public was a classic in pseudologic.

There was no mention made of the Bower-Gray confession. Instead, the board members gave as their reason for commutation the results of a ballistics experiment they had conducted. In their presence one hundred .44-caliber shells had been test fired from a .45 revolver. A few of the shells ruptured; all of them swelled out. The .44 shell found at the scene of the murder had not swelled out and could easily be reinserted in a .44 cylinder. Thus, reasoned the board, inasmuch as Davis was known to have been carrying a .45 revolver, he could not have fired the .44 slugs which killed the herders since only a .44 could have fired them.

In essence the board was saying, "Since Diamondfield Jack could not have killed the herders, we will now commute his death sentence to life imprisonment." While Hawley was gratified to know that Davis would live, he was hardly satisfied with the logic of the pardon board. He began to plan another appeal to the state Supreme Court.

Davis was immediately moved again to the penitentiary to begin serving his life sentence. It was an emotional moment when Diamondfield Jack left the jail in Albion for the trip to Boise. Sheriff Adams gave him a gold watch, symbolic of the friendship of the community toward the man they had once railroaded to the gallows, and treated him to a particularly fine dinner in his cell. Scores of people dropped by the jail to say goodbye, a number of them bringing small presents to the prisoner. Davis now knew for the first time that he would not be executed.

Within a few months after his arrival in Boise a new danger developed—the possibility that lack of interest and buck-passing would prevent the courts or the pardon board from dealing with Davis' case, now that it was no longer a life-and-death matter. People who had been key participants in the events of the last six years and were vitally interested in it were now no longer involved in the case. O. W. Powers was in the Utah legislature, and had just declined an appointment to the U.S. Senate. Rogers and Borah were back practicing law. K. I. Perky had become a district judge. John Sparks was getting interested in Nevada politics, and had sold his interest in the cattle corporation. J. W. Dorsey, the polished San Francisco counsel for Sparks-Harrell, took on more and more of the legal burden, with Hawley and Puckett assuming less and less. Hawley decided to run for mayor of Boise.

Dorsey kept in touch with Jack Davis regularly. With one letter he enclosed a clipping from the fashionable *Sunset* magazine describing the annual hunt on the Sparks-Harrell ranches. It was described in terms that made it seem like the hunt of a feudal manor. Among the aristocrats mentioned and pictured in the article, Sparks and Harrell were clearly recognizable, but the references to Bower and Gray did not make it clear whether they were serfs or sires of the estate. In any event, Jack Davis must have resented deeply the snug little Sparks-Harrell crowd enjoying life while continuing to provide for the two men who were the real killers.

Meanwhile, Hawley apparently recognized the increasing danger of apathy and indifference. He turned once more to the Idaho Supreme Court, determined to goad the justices into some kind of intervention into what was obviously a miscarriage of justice. Late in 1901 Hawley argued hypothetically before this court that even if Wilson and Cummings were to turn up alive the courts seemed powerless to disturb Davis' conviction. Justice Stockslager participated in the decision, even though he had been the judge in the original trial. To Hawley's chagrin, the Supreme Court agreed. The decision, written by Justice Quarles, noted:

The able and eloquent counsel for the appellant insists that under the provisions of our criminal laws, as they exist in this State to-day, that "A" might be convicted of the crime of the murder of "B" and sentenced to a term of imprisonment for life, and one year afterwards "B" might turn up alive and walk into the Court which tried and sentenced "A", and that the Court would be powerless to grant to "A" a new trial. This contention of the able counsel is correct, but the picture which he presents is so overdrawn that there is no danger of its occurring one time in a thousand years. Again the case presented by this overdrawn picture presupposes the conviction of "A" without proof of the *corpus delecti,* which could hardly occur in any civilized country. But, in the event of such case, while the power to grant relief does not rest with the Courts, yet our Constitution has vested the power of granting relief to another tribunal, to wit: the Board of Pardons.[3]

Thus, there was now nothing else to do but go back to the pardon board in an effort to obtain the full clemency that seemed to be justified by the logic of the board's commutation decision. Fortunately for

Hawley and his client, Hunt's Democratic administration seemed to enjoy its new power as a pardon board. But unfortunately, for men who had been elected by a slim margin, the three officials did not always consider the consequences of their acts. In 1901 they pardoned a number of the miners who had been imprisoned as a result of the Coeur d'Alene mining troubles of 1899. Included among this group was Paul Corcoran, the union official whom Hawley and Borah had worked so hard to convict as a demonstration to the world that the union itself was responsible to the law for the acts of its members. Corcoran's imprisonment had literally been the symbol of the triumph of "law and order" in Idaho.

Public reaction was highly critical of this large-scale pardon and parole movement. Newspapers editorialized that Governor Hunt was emptying the prison, and that he was violating his oath of office by turning loose the "dynamiters" in an effort to woo the labor vote of northern Idaho. Many people generalized that the Governor was soft on crime. Credence was given to rumors that John Sparks would succeed in buying a pardon for Diamondfield Jack from Hunt, and that he had tried without success to buy Davis' freedom from Governor Steunenberg two years earlier.[4] It was a confused situation for Hawley; never had the chance of getting a pardon looked so good, but never had the public reaction to pardons looked quite so hostile. Hunt's ineptness on the parole issue, along with the shrill criticism of the *Idaho Statesman,* kept the public aroused on the subject of criminals, and while Davis was in prison he was still a criminal—even though the overwhelming bulk of the evidence showed him innocent.

By mid-1902 it looked as if the Hunt administration had committed a bad political error. Attorney General Martin decided not to seek reelection that fall, but Hunt and Bassett bravely decided to run again. They even scheduled a meeting of the pardon board for the fall of 1902, coinciding with the time of the campaign and election.

In November the voters repudiated the Hunt administration. Hunt was decisively defeated by the Republican John T. Morrison and Bassett lost to Wilmot H. Gibson. While it would be unwise to attribute their defeat primarily to the pardon issue, it was certainly a factor. It is true that there had been a general swing back toward the Republican party in Idaho after the silver issue died down. But this movement was neither a regional reflection of Theodore Roosevelt's national popularity nor a silver state economic phenomenon— as witnessed by the fact that in Nevada that year John Sparks, a Democrat, was elected governor by a sizeable margin. It is reasonable to assume that the law and order issue served as the "clincher" in the Idaho elections.

In the waning days of 1902 the Idaho Board of Pardons was a lame-duck agency. Still, the three men officially had the power of pardon and parole. In the face of continued public criticism they went on with their hearings in November and December of 1902. Hawley seized the opportunity; he worked up one final set of statements from the key figures of the whole affair: his own views, plus those of Davis, Rogers, Powers, Bower, the Cassia County ranchers, Sparks, Harrell, Dorsey, *et al.*

It was, however, a delicate situation in many ways. Even though the evidence and logic were on Davis' side and a number of important men of prestige were testifying in his behalf, there was always the reality that it was a repudiated state administration which would have to grant the pardon. And the action would be in the face of enormous public hostility to leniency toward criminals. Then, too, certain individuals had to protect their own public image—particularly John Sparks who was now being called "Honest John" by his political supporters in Nevada. "Honest John" Sparks would have to explain—for the first time in the public limelight—how he stood silent, knowing the facts of the case, for so long.

Sparks deposed once more to the board how Bower had found him in Ogden on February 8, 1896, and told him of the shooting, how Bower had talked of leaving the country, and how he, Sparks, had convinced him that he should not. Explaining his own silence in the matter, Sparks said,

I was greatly in doubt as to my duty in the matter. I regarded the statement made to me by Mr. Bower as the confidential utterances of a friend. I did not believe from the statement made that a crime had been committed as the circumstances seemed to warrant Gray's apparent belief that his own life and Bower's were in danger when he fired the shots. I realized however that there was great excitement in regard to the matter and grave danger; therefore, if the parties were tried I felt assured also that if the matter became public it would ruin Bower and his family. Both Mr. Harrell and myself concluded that the proper course to pursue was to keep silent as to our knowledge of the affair; not, however, with any intention of concealing the matter from the authorities, or of protecting any person charged with or who had committed a crime, because I firmly intended if questioned by any one who had authority so to do with reference to the matter to make a full statement in regard to it.

Sparks concluded by saying,

When Gleason and Davis were arrested in 1897 and charged with the murder of Wilson and Cummings my proper course in the matter became a matter of still graver doubt with me. Both men had worked for my company but outside of that I had no interest in either. I knew both of them were innocent but could not make my knowledge public without violating the confidence that had been placed in me by Bower. Neither Bower nor Gray seemed willing to make public their connection with the affair. I did not believe it possible to convict innocent men and was unwilling to betray the confidence of a friend unless it became my legal duty to impart my knowledge of the matter. I talked the matter over with Bower. He assured me that he would in the event of a conviction of either Davis or Gleason make the whole matter public, that he would never see an innocent man punished. I concluded my proper course was to defend the accused men. This Mr. Harrell and myself have continued to do from the inception of the cases against Davis and Gleason up to the present time.[5]

Many of the other depositions were essentially restatements of what the board had heard before. Most were relatively brief; a few were powerful pieces of persuasion. Perhaps the most effective presentation came from the johnny-come-lately of the case, J. W. Dorsey, the Sparks-Harrell attorney. With moving eloquence and compelling logic he first identified himself to these Idaho officials—not as a San Francisco corporation lawyer, but as a man of the saddle and western courtroom, a true "sagebrush lawyer." He then indicated why he had become convinced that Davis was not guilty. His colorful statement follows:

I am an attorney at law, and as such have been engaged in active general practice of my profession for more than twenty-five years. I have been the District Attorney of Elko County, Nevada, during two terms, and for about fourteen years was employed in either the prosecution or defense of nearly every important criminal case tried in that County.

I have hunted upon and travelled over the range of the Sparks-Harrell Company a great many times. For years I was a member of an annual hunting party upon that range. For years I have been the attorney for the company, and I have frequently been professionally employed in and about the private business, and have been a frequent visitor at the homes of Mr. John Sparks and Mr. Andrew Harrell, respectively the President and Secretary of the Company. They are my warm, personal friends.

I was first employed in behalf of Jack Davis in the early part of the year 1899; and thereafter until July, 1901, almost constantly I was engaged in the examination, preparation, or trial of some branch of the case which involved the investigation of the facts, motions for new trials, writs of habeas corpus, appeals, and applications for a pardon or commutation of sentence. I have repeatedly interviewed Jack Davis personally, and have heard his story from every point of view which my experience and desire to learn everything touching, or possibly bearing upon the question of his guilt or innocence, suggested.

I have received from him many letters embracing every phase of the inquiry—many of them of great length and of minute detail, one of them covering one hundred twenty typewritten pages of legal cap when I had it copied. I have camped, hunted, ridden, and driven with James E. Bower and Jeff D. Gray, and have heard each of them, over and over again, from every conceivable standpoint—on the witness stand in the crowded court room, in professional interview and under stress of the most searching and critical cross examination, in narrative form while hunting in the mountains and while driving along the public highway, in the presence of others, and in private interviews, consultation, and discussion—tell his story of the killing of John C. Wilson and Daniel Cummings. I have carefully and many times from differing premises examined Buck Rice, J. P. Duncan, A. D. Norton, Henry Jones, C. H. Hewett, and Henry Harris, upon the subject of Jeff Gray's confession immediately after the killing that he killed both Wilson and Cummings. I assisted in the defense of Gray at his trial during the February, 1899, term of the District Court of Cassia County, for the killing of Wilson, and heard the testimony establishing the fact that he personally, on February 4, 1896, killed both Wilson and Cummings, and I saw him acquitted upon the ground of self-defense, and subsequently heard a number of the jurymen who tried him say that they were convinced that Gray alone committed the homicide and that he did it to save his own life and that of Bower's. I know the story, from James E. Bower and John Sparks, of how Bower travelled from the scene of the shooting to the Point-of-the-Mountain ranch, from there to the HD ranch, from there to Wells, and thence to Reno, to find and tell John Sparks, the President of his company, how Wilson and Cummings came to their death; how he learned at Reno that Mr. Sparks had started East the day before with a train load of cattle, and how Bower followed him and caught him at Ogden on the morning of February 9th (I think) and told him all about the trouble with Wilson and Cummings and how Gray had shot them both.

I have time and time again discussed the question of the guilt or innocence of Jack Davis with John C. Rogers, the District Attorney of Cassia County, who filed the information against and had charge of the prosecution of Davis for the killing of Wilson, and have heard him give the reasons why he had first believed Davis guilty and how he gradually, after the conviction of Davis and after the admissions of Bower and Gray, grew doubtful and more doubtful upon the subject of the guilt of Davis, until finally in the light of the facts subsequently ascertained he became convinced that Davis had nothing to do with the crime charged against him. I have heard Judge O. W. Powers, who assisted Mr. Rogers in the prosecution of Davis and whose ripe experience in criminal cases and rare eloquence contributed largely toward the conviction, express the gravest doubts of the justice of Davis's conviction, and his absolute belief that Davis should not and could not have been convicted if Bower and Gray had come forward and testified at his trial to the facts subsequently admitted by them. I have talked upon the subject of Davis's guilt with the sheriffs and officers who had him in charge from the time of his conviction until the commutation of his sentence in 1901—who heard the witnesses in the case tell their stories in and out of court, who knew Davis intimately, and were familiar with every circumstance in the case from information gathered from every possible source—and I have heard them state their belief in his innocence. I am aware that Davis carried a .45 caliber pistol and that the empty shells found on the ground near the wagon of the dead sheepherders were of .44 caliber, and I am informed and believe that numerous experiments have demonstrated that a .44 shell cannot be discharged from a .45 revolver and again inserted (without great difficulty—if at all) in the chamber of a .44 pistol. I understand that the .44 shell found at the wagon can be readily inserted in a .44 pistol.

I mentioned the foregoing facts merely to indicate the period and character of my professional experience, my familiarity with the range and its management, the intimate relationship which has existed for many years between the officers of the corporate owners and myself, to show the sort of interest I have been compelled to take in the case, my opportunities for ascertaining the truth, and the source, kind, and quality of the evidence upon which I relied in forming my belief as to the guilt or innocence of Jack Davis. Everything I know and have heard strengthens my belief in his innocence of the killing of Wilson and Cummings, or either.

I do not believe that any man of the attainments and in the position of Davis could have said and written what he did to me and be guilty. I regard everything he has said and written as consistent with innocence and inconsistent with guilt. He has in every manner reviled Bower and Gray for their delay in confessing their connection with the killing of the sheep men. I do not believe he would have dared to so risk their enmity and abandonment if he were guilty. In my judgment he has been far too talkative and outspoken—too abusive of those whose withdrawal of support would leave him helpless—to have committed the crime charged against him. To my mind it is incredible that James E. Bower, a well known and reputable citizen of Cassia County, a man of property and standing in the community—who knew that a dominant industry in Cassia County is sheep raising, and that sheepmen would probably constitute a majority of any jury that could be empaneled, and would be glad to find any reasonable ground for fastening guilt upon a cattleman —would have jeopardized his fortune, family, and life for Jack Davis under any other circumstances than such as has been related by him. And it is impossible that Jeff Gray, between whom and Davis no friendship has ever existed, who was not even in the employ of the Sparks-Harrell Company, would risk his life to save that of a man he scarcely knew and for whom he has no love. No other theory than that of implicit belief in the innocence of Davis could have enlisted the active sympathy and generous support of men like John Sparks and Andrew J. Harrell—men of the highest character and position, one of them now the Governor-elect of the State of Nevada. Their personal knowledge of the character of the country over which Davis must have ridden if he had been a party to the homicide, and the distances he must have covered within the time fixed by his known presence at various times on the range, their familiar acquaintance with Rice, Duncan, Norton, Jones, Hewett, and Harris, and the improbability that these men would attempt to falsely fasten the killing upon Gray (who was the brother-in-law of Jones, the employee of Norton, and who had worked for Hewett and with Harris, and was an old acquaintance of Duncan and Rice, and the friend of them all), the long journey taken by Bower to find Mr. Sparks immediately after the killing, and his confession to Sparks at Ogden the moment he overtook him, the subsequent confession of Gray to Mr. Sparks—in short, their unbounded opportunities for getting at the facts and sifting out the truth, the fact that they were repositories of a secret which during that period of intense feeling and bitter animosity must be preserved because it jeopardized the lives of two men—Bower and Gray, their unswerving belief in the innocence of Davis and the loyal, disinterested, and open-handed assistance which they have extended to him—have created, with the other facts and circumstances I have stated, a profound belief to my mind of the strength and certainty of a mathematical demonstration that Jack Davis had nothing whatever to do with the killing of Wilson and Cummings, or of either of them, by his own act, or by any sort of participation, conspiracy, foreknowledge or otherwise.

With a full understanding of all the obligations of an oath, under the laws of God and man, I solemnly affirm that I believe Jack Davis is as innocent of the crime for which he was tried and of which he was convicted as I am, or as is any member of this Board of Pardons.

San Francisco   J. W. Dorsey[6]
November 22, 1902

In reply to this eloquent and logical plea by Dorsey there was just one voice raised before the pardon board. Against the chorus of prominent people seeking freedom for Davis, William E. Borah truculently, and without supporting evidence, argued that the prosecution of Davis had been proper and just from the very beginning. Said he, on December 13, 1902:

Gentlemen:

Before the matter of the pardon of Jack Davis is passed upon, I desire that the board be not misled by a report which seems to have been given credence by some and possibly all of the members of the board—that is, that all who were connected with the prosecution are satisfied that Davis is innocent. It is but fair to say to the board that this is wholly an error. It is quite true that some who were at one time excessive in their zeal to prosecute have been permitted to see new light and are quite as excessive now in their zeal to release Mr. Davis. Knowing as I do the facts in the case and knowing as I do also that some of these men know them, I have no explanation to make with reference to this change of position. I presume the charitable view to take of that matter is that they would rather see ninety and nine guilty men escape than to see one innocent man suffer (under certain circumstances.)

I have not been connected with this matter professionally for a long time but I have kept up an interest in the case and have watched closely the testimony in the case, and I desire to say to the board that I have not at this time one particle of doubt as to the fact that Jack Davis murdered

Cummins [*sic*] and Wilson. I believe, too, that it was a crime wholly without extenuation, that it was boasted of repeatedly by the wretch who did it, openly talked of by him and his friends days before the world at large knew anything about it, proven at the trial beyond a doubt, and never yet have the prominent facts of the case been changed, explained or modified to my mind. I do not contend for a moment that Bower did not assist. He did assist. We knew this all the time. The entire prosecution knew it but we were unable to proceed at that time because we could not close up some of the links in the chain owing to the fact that he most cautiously covered up his tracks. But he did not assist in the manner which he now states.

I am aware that I will likely be charged with prejudice and vindictiveness but I disclaim both. I simply know what I am talking about and I do not want it understood that the rumor that those connected with the prosecution have changed their views has any verity in it so far as I am concerned. I am not going to review the evidence, nor present any argument against his pardon; that is not the purpose of this letter, and all this has been gone over before. I submit this statement for what it is worth.

Very respectfully,

W. E. Borah[7]

Borah as the last hold-out of the prosecution staff may have been badly outnumbered in his attempts to get the board to stand firmly against pardon, but he was by no means the only voice of protest. The *Idaho Statesman* also continued to hammer away against the Hunt administration and the possibility of a pardon for Diamondfield Jack.

On December 17, 1902, Hawley thought he saw indications that the pardon board was weakening. He wrote to John Sparks, reporting that the possibility of a pardon was now imminent but that anything could yet happen with such a vacillating group of men. Hawley, who was normally tolerant of human frailty, was highly critical of the three members of the pardon board. He told Sparks, "I hope never again to be compelled to deal with such a lot of small caliber men in high positions."

Later that same day the Board of Pardons met— for what was to be its final meeting in the case of Jack Davis. Hawley's hunch was correct. By a two to one vote the board granted Diamondfield Jack his pardon. Governor Hunt and Secretary of State Bassett voted in favor of pardon; Attorney General Martin voted against Davis.

There was certainly bound to be trouble when the *Statesman*—the "morning mummy"—learned of the pardon. James Hawley quickly talked with his friends on the afternoon *Capital News,* and reported the results of the conversation in another letter to his client, John Sparks:

> I have made arrangements with the Evening Capital News to defend the Board against the attacks of the Statesman and the Bulletin. This was something that had to be done. I do not apprehend a great deal of trouble, but we will certainly have some. To a great extent it has been caused by Hunt's vacillating course. If the pardon had been granted when it should have been, right immediately following the argument on this last application, there would have been far less talk and suspicion of wrong doing than there is now.[8]

Hawley's anticipation of the reaction proved well-founded. The *Statesman* was furious when it learned of the pardon, and on the following morning it railed editorially against Diamondfield Jack Davis, Governor Hunt, the cattlemen, and the defense. In a style remarkably akin to that of Borah the newspaper said:

The board of pardons has liberated "Diamondfield Jack" Davis. This result was not unexpected. For nearly two years it has been anticipated. Ever since the recklessness of the majority of the board was demonstrated the public has been prepared for this pardon. It knew what influences were at work and with such a board, it did not seem possible that those influences would fail to bring about a result of this character. Still, there were a great many who hoped that this last disgrace would not be inflicted upon the state. . . . But that hope has been dashed to the ground and the state bows its head, oppressed by a sense of outrage and disgrace.

This action by the board is far reaching; it is a menace to our institutions. When a board of pardons will thus overthrow the decrees of the courts without any reasonable excuse, releasing a murderer solely because wealthy friends have conjured up a filmy explanation as an excuse for pardoning the convict, the very foundations of the temple of justice are threatened.

The chapter is closed so far as official action is concerned. It will no longer have additions in the form of new developments, but it will not be forgotten by the people, because they feel that a high trust has been violated in a manner so scandalous that it constitutes a lasting reproach on the commonwealth.[9]

Frank Martin, like an earlier attorney general, R. E. McFarland, who had vocally dissented against any reprieves for Diamondfield Jack several years earlier, now issued a strongly worded statement to the press indicating that the pardon was a gross miscarriage of justice—inasmuch as all the legal reviews and appeals still upheld the original conviction. The *Statesman* also reran Borah's earlier statement to the board in which he had truculently—and almost intuitively—insisted that Davis was still guilty.

Newspaper reporters tried to get statements from Governor Hunt and Secretary of State Bassett, but both men were reluctant to comment on their vote to free Davis. Hunt was quoted as saying, cryptically, that "he thought Diamondfield Jack was in the wrong place." In an unguarded moment he also told a reporter that he originally thought that Davis was guilty, and had changed his mind only when he (Hunt) had become better acquainted with Governor Sparks.[10] Gleefully the editorial critics seized upon this last remark to conclude that Sparks had indeed bought the pardon. Estimates of the money Sparks had spent varied from $30,000 to $100,000, and one writer let his imagination—or his decimal point—get away from him when he surmised that $1,000,000 was involved.[11] Small-town newspapers around Idaho picked up the chant, "miscarriage of justice," and it became obvious from newspaper editorials that the timing of the pardon had been unfortunate—coming, as it did, as a climax to the Hunt administration's pardoning spree.

But overlooked by the newspaper editors in the furor of Davis' release was the fact that an overwhelming body of evidence and two confessions supported his innocence, and that he had spent six years in jail for a crime he probably did not commit. The whole affair had taken on political overtones long before, rather than remaining a case in law. A curious alliance of the sheepmen, the Democratic state administration, the Republican *Statesman,* and Borah had seemed determined that Davis would hang, regardless of considerable new light which had been cast on the case since the original conviction. After 1898 it should have been clear that Diamondfield Jack's greatest crime in Idaho was in being a braggart and a bully. But the alliance had wanted him executed nonetheless. It would strengthen their position if they could make the original prosecution story stick, but now it would embarrass them if they had to accept the Bower-Gray story. Thus, it was somewhat easier for the *Statesman* and other papers to cry for "law and order" rather than to cry for "justice" in the case of Davis.

Diamondfield Jack Davis walked out of the Idaho penitentiary a free man on December 18, 1902. He was decked out in freshly pressed clothes (the *Statesman* even saw in the fact that the clothes had gone to the cleaner a week earlier the existence of a "deal" to release Davis), given the $10.55 he had on the books, and cordially sent on his way by prisoners and guards. A buggy was sent out to bring him into downtown Boise, some two miles west on Warm Springs Avenue. But Davis stopped the buggy at the eastern edge of town at the famous Natatorium, an elegant resort known far and wide throughout the West for its hot-water pool and its well-appointed bar. Here, in this improbable locale, Jack Davis tasted his first freedom. Never a man for drinking alone, Davis was happy that James Hawley—the persistent and resourceful attorney

who had saved his life, and now mayor-elect of Boise—
came out from town and had a few drinks with him.

The two men must have made a strange picture at
the bar. Hawley was an impressive figure—six feet four
inches tall, weighing well over two hundred pounds,
and carrying his fifty-five years with considerable dig-
nity. By contrast, Davis stood five feet seven inches,
and weighed 150 pounds. Although he was still only
thirty-one years old, six years and eight months behind
bars had taken the ruddy hue from his complexion,
and he no longer looked the part of the hired gunman
who had once terrorized Cassia County. Gone, too,
was much of the brashness; he bluntly expressed his
gratitude to Hawley and agreed with the attorney's sug-
gestion that he get out of the state promptly and stay out.

That night Davis checked into the Overland Hotel in
Boise. In the morning critical newspapers indignantly
reported the scene at the Natatorium the previous afternoon, describing how one of Idaho's most respectable
citizens, the next mayor of Boise, had brazenly been
drinking with one of Idaho's most disreputable criminals. But neither Hawley nor Davis, it seems certain,
gave a thought to the latest newspaper attacks on them.
The whole messy episode was over at last, and life
could now go on.

Later that same day Jack Davis, considerably older
and wiser than he had been when he first came to the
state ten years earlier, went to the Boise railroad depot
to begin his first journey in freedom since he had fled
southward in 1896. There, announcing to reporters
that he intended to start life anew in the mining camp

of Tonopah, Nevada, Diamondfield Jack boarded a train and left Idaho forever.

NOTES

[1]*Idaho Statesman,* July 14, 1901.
[2]*Evening Capital News,* July 15, 1901.
[3]*State* v. *Davis,* 8 Idaho 115.
[4]The rumors concerning the alleged bribes were mentioned in Idaho newspapers at the time, and are reported in the W.P.A. book *Idaho Lore.*
[5]Sparks' deposition is in the Hawley papers.
[6]Dorsey's statement is in the Hawley papers.
[7]Borah's letter to the Board of Pardons is in the Hawley papers.
[8]Hawley's letters to Sparks, dated December 17, 1902, are in the correspondence files of the Hawley papers.
[9]*Idaho Statesman,* December 18, 1902.
[10]*Idaho Statesman,* 1902; undated clipping in the scrapbook collection of the Hawley papers.
[11]*Ibid.*

The Aftermath

WHAT DID IT ALL MEAN—the chain of events from 1896 through 1902 which saw the state of Idaho's prosecution of Diamondfield Jack turn into a rancorous political battle? Who was to blame for the "Code of the West" justice which twice took Davis to the gallows, and which kept him imprisoned even after conceding his innocence?

Responsibility for the situation has to be shared by a great many Idaho people, groups, and institutions. Certainly the Board of Pardons must be singled out as a group of men lacking in courage, legal ability, and common sense, after they repeatedly chose to overlook the mountain of evidence and the two confessions which supported Davis' innocence. The sheep raisers must be criticized, too, for the blindness and vindictiveness of their position; their attorney, William E. Borah, in the face of overwhelming evidence to the contrary still wanted the scalp of Diamondfield Jack, long after all of his legal colleagues had changed their

minds. By the same token, John Sparks and the cattlemen must be criticized for their suppression of truth
and for their protection of the guilty men, even though
they were simultaneously providing for the defense of
the innocent victim, Davis. Also, the moderation of
public opinion might have permitted the satisfactory
resolution of the case two years earlier had it not been
for the indignant and ill-timed outcries of the *Idaho
Statesman,* the most influential newspaper in the state.

Even the political parties have to assume some of
the blame for the confused situation. The Republicans,
particularly in 1902, in using the "law and order"
issue made it appear that the release of any imprisoned
man by a Democratic administration was a sign of
softness and irresponsibility by the party in power. By
the same token, the extremely bad timing and the ineptness of the Democratic administration caused the
real issues of the case to be forgotten in the passions of
the moment. Furthermore, the introduction of the religious issue by political opportunists certainly did not
help the cause of calmness and justice, since anti-
Mormonism was still a sensitive issue within the state.

The courts, too, might have done a better job of
dispensing justice. At the time that the Idaho Supreme
Court denied a new trial in 1898 it was clear that the
justices had accepted a completely circumstantial explanation of the case. When one of the key circumstances—the murder ride—was later shown to be
virtually impossible, the court's only answer was that
it was now too late to grant a new trial. Moreover,
Justice Stockslager's failure to disqualify himself in

ruling on a case in which he had been the lower court judge raises a question of professional ethics.

Certain basic weaknesses in Idaho's legal system clearly emerged from the case. As early as 1901 the *Evening Capital News* of Boise had pointed out that new evidence, discovered after the ten-day period in which requests for new trials must be initiated, could have absolutely no effect on the course of justice. A pardon board might use the evidence as a basis for commutation or pardon, but this procedure would not legally clear a man's name; instead, it would represent a pardon for a crime of which the man was still officially guilty.

Happily, however, considerable good seems to have come out of the whole Diamondfield Jack affair. Many of the difficulties cited above were obvious to the people of the state, who must have felt conscience-stricken as they watched justice reach a new nadir in Idaho. For, a few years later, during the famous Haywood trial in Boise in 1907—when the hatred and passions of the past were the very theme of the trial—Idaho demonstrated to the nation and the world that she could, under the most trying circumstances, administer her laws calmly and fairly.

Legal historians might be tempted to draw several different conclusions from the Diamondfield Jack case. To some, the case would stand as a conspicuous example of the unevenness of justice on a frontier that clung to "Code of the West" justice longer than it would be willing to admit. To others it might even be viewed as another Dreyfuss case. But the passing of time, and the passing away of all the principal figures of the case, have taken away much of the sting of injustice. Long ago the memory of Idaho's ineptness in handling the case and the resultant public disillusionment disappeared from the social conscience of the intermountain West. To those who followed the events of 1896 through 1902 with concern, the fact that the quality of justice in Idaho improved sharply in the succeeding years argued that no real and permanent wrong had been done. Likewise, when Jack Davis later experienced good fortune in Nevada after his misfortunes in Idaho, the pangs of conscience were softened for those who had been parties to the kind of justice dispensed in turn-of-the-century Idaho.

Even in law and legal history there is a place for the pragmatic view. James H. Hawley, who, probably more than any other man, was responsible for a stable and law-abiding society in Idaho, had a near-obsession about the importance of the law, but he tempered this feeling with a pragmatism which shaped his interpretation of the law.[1] From this vantage point Hawley apparently felt that the outcome of the Diamondfield Jack case was entirely satisfactory.

Moreover, the bitter animosity between sheepmen and cattlemen in Idaho eased somewhat as a result of the affair in Cassia County. John MacLane, in his biography of Hawley entitled *A Sagebrush Lawyer,* concludes that a "*modus vivendi* between the sheep and cattle men" grew out of it, and that "both sheep and cattle men accepted the situation, and carried on their respective businesses in peace and amity." Edward N.

Wentworth, in *America's Sheep Trails,* says that the incident caused the cattle barons to reassess their position, and to exhibit a more tolerant attitude toward the sheepmen. Perhaps, but a procattlemen historian might draw the opposite conclusion—that the incident showed to the world that the cattlemen were not the only aggressors in the range wars of the West. Regardless of the outcome, both sides have ample reason to want to forget the whole episode. But feeling dies slowly. In Cassia County and Twin Falls County, which was carved out of Cassia County in 1907, there is still a strong reluctance to discuss the case since many direct relatives of prominent participants—and partisans—still remain.

Physically the country has not changed much in the ensuing sixty-five years, except along the south edge of the Snake River where an enormous reclamation project has created a rich agricultural area. The rest of the area remains much as it was at the time Diamondfield Jack rode the range. A railroad and a paved highway run south now from the Snake River to the Humboldt River along the chain of ranches once belonging to Sparks-Harrell, but, except for a colorful gambling settlement at the state line, the range looks much the same as it did in 1896 when the great ranch empire controlled it. The crumbling remains of the Middlestacks ranch still stand on the Nevada side of the line. The Brown ranch is gone, buried under many feet of water in what is now the Salmon Creek Reservoir, so no researcher will ever be able to determine the time of sunrise there in early February. But other landmarks near the scene of the murder remain—the Point ranch and Buck Rice's place, sentinel outposts in what is still today lonely rangeland.

The eastern side of the county remains equally unchanged. In fact, it may have drifted backward—particularly in the case of Albion. When irrigation brought prosperity to the flat land along the Snake River, Albion watched helplessly as the county seat was moved down to Burley. A final blow to the little community came in the mid 1950's, when the state normal school which had been there since the 1890's was closed in an economy move. Albion became almost a ghost town; today while Burley is a thriving and prosperous small city, Albion lies forgotten, many buildings abandoned, in the high valley only fifteen miles away. The old frame courthouse still stands as a silent memorial to the great drama that was once enacted there, but the sleepy little community at the foot of the high ridge where snow stands all summer looks like the last place in the world in which it could have happened.

But the effects of a legal and political struggle such as the Diamondfield Jack affair are much more noticeable on people than they are on geographical areas. Some of the men who played prominent roles in the case went on to greatness in other places and other times: two became governors, and two became United States senators. Others quietly slipped back into the serenity and obscurity of daily life in Cassia County.

Of all the people in the Diamondfield Jack case, William E. Borah gained the most fame and prestige from his participation. His role in the case and his

participation with Hawley in the 1899 riot cases cata-
pulted him into prominence in legal and political circles
of the state. In 1906, when Governor Steunenberg was
assassinated (apparently in retaliation for sending
troops to quell the labor disturbances in northern
Idaho in 1899), Borah and Hawley again teamed up
in the Haywood trial.[2] During the preparation of this
case Borah's fame as a prosecutor won him election to
the United States Senate by the Idaho legislature. Before this case was over, however, and before he took
his seat in the Senate, Borah's reputation was momentarily tarnished when he was indicted by a federal
grand jury for land fraud. Borah considered resigning
from the Senate, but finally decided to fight the indictment. With Hawley as his lawyer, Borah won an
acquittal and triumphantly went to Washington in the
fall of 1907. There he spent the rest of his lifetime as
one of the most distinguished members of the Senate.
The "Lone Lion of Idaho" died there in 1940, still
displaying the independent attitude that characterized
his role in the closing days of the Diamondfield Jack
case.

James H. Hawley likewise enhanced his enormous
popularity throughout the state by his courageous and
persistent efforts in the Diamondfield Jack case. At the
end of his term as mayor of Boise he became senior
counsel for the state in the prosecution of Bill Haywood for the Steunenberg murder. Even though most
accounts of the Haywood trial tend to emphasize
Borah's role, it was really Hawley who directed the
work of the prosecution. Although Haywood was even-

tually acquitted, Hawley was able to realize his larger purpose in the trial—the reformation of the miners' union into a law-abiding organization. Always a popular figure in the state, Hawley was elected governor in 1910, but he was never able to achieve his one great dream—serving in the United States Senate. He died in Boise in 1929, universally praised as one of the great pioneers of the state of Idaho.

Kirtland I. Perky, Hawley's colleague in the defense of Davis, went on to prominence as a district judge in Idaho, and later, for a brief time, as a United States Senator when Governor Hawley appointed him to fill the unexpired term of Senator Heyburn, who died in 1912. Perky also achieved some degree of fame—or perhaps notoriety in conservative Idaho—when he played host to Clarence Darrow while the great criminal lawyer was in Boise for the Haywood trial. In the 1920's Perky moved to California; he died in Long Beach in 1939.

Orlando W. Powers, the prosecution attorney, returned to his law practice in Salt Lake City. Although he had declined an appointment to the U.S. Senate in 1900, he, like Hawley, wanted to arrive in that body on his own. To that end, he remained active politically, and in 1908 as head of the Utah delegation to the Democratic National Convention he seconded the presidential nomination of Perky's onetime law partner— William Jennings Bryan. In 1911 Powers ran for the U.S. Senate, but, like Hawley, he discovered that the odds were too high for a Democrat in a state which was primarily Republican. He died in Salt Lake City in 1914.

The other prosecution attorney, John C. Rogers, moved to the new metropolis of Burley, where he became the first practicing attorney. Presumably his practice was never again as colorful and exciting as it was during the Diamondfield Jack affair. James E. Bower and Jeff Gray stayed on in Cassia and Twin Falls counties; the presence of their descendants there today makes the whole episode a sensitive and touchy subject which is not often discussed.

The first of the key figures of the case to die were the Harrells, with the father passing away in 1901, and the son in 1907. John Sparks' remaining years were almost as brief. In 1906 he was reelected Governor of Nevada for a second four-year term, but a series of labor troubles in Goldfield, generated by the Western Federation of Miners and the newly-founded Industrial Workers of the World (the Wobblies), gave Governor Sparks a great deal of trouble. After first utilizing local strong men, including his old Cassia County terror, Diamondfield Jack, Sparks finally felt compelled to ask for federal troops to help maintain law and order. President Theodore Roosevelt complied with Sparks' request, but then decided there never had been any need for the federal troops in the first place, and hastily withdrew them. The stress of events was too much for Sparks: he became ill during the Goldfield troubles, and died near Reno in May of 1908 in the middle of his second term in office. One of his biographers maintains that he "died of a broken heart" caused by Roosevelt's rebuff.[3]

During those tense days of 1907 which had broken

---

the health and spirit of Governor Sparks, Diamondfield Jack Davis had been in Goldfield. How he got there, and what he was doing there, makes an interesting sequel to the gunman's career in Idaho and to our now-completed study in frontier justice.

NOTES

[1] For Hawley's role in "civilizing" Idaho, see Albert Lewis' unpublished paper "Sagebrush Rhetoric: The Oratory of James H. Hawley." For Hawley's pragmatism see David H. Grover, "James H. Hawley, Pioneer Persuader and Pragmatist," *Western Speech,* Winter, 1966.

[2] For Borah and Hawley's role in the events of 1906–1907, see David H. Grover, *Debaters and Dynamiters: The Story of the Haywood Trial.*

[3] The source for the statement about the "broken heart" of John Sparks was Mrs. Velma Stevens Truett of Elko, Nevada.

Sequel

A FEW DAYS after leaving Boise at the end of 1902, Diamondfield Jack Davis turned up in Tonopah, Nevada, to begin an episode just as flamboyant as the one that had gone before. Facts concerning this period of his life are incomplete, but there are enough newspaper accounts from the Nevada mining camps to give us some idea of the remarkable change of fortune which Jack Davis encountered in the next few years.

Davis had been a miner once before and the faraway lure of mineral wealth still appealed to him, so it was natural that he was attracted to this last great American mining boom in search of money and a new start in life. In Tonopah, early in 1903, after an unsuccessful attempt at claim-jumping, he persuaded George Wingfield and J. L. Ford to stake him to a prospector's outfit, and he immediately struck out for the desert. When money got low he obtained additional capital from George S. Nixon of Winnemucca, a banker who was interested in good mining prospects, and from his old courtroom adversary-turned-friend, Judge O. W. Powers of Salt Lake City.

Within a short period of time Diamondfield Jack had located a number of first-rate claims, reportedly including such soon-to-be-famous properties as the Daisy, Quartette, Black Butte, Belmont, and Eureka. His most important holdings were near Diamondfield, a town he founded some four miles east of Goldfield. In addition, he had dozens of properties in such camps as Bullfrog, Goldreed, and Goldflat, and he operated two fourteen-horse freight teams between Diamondfield and Goldfield. He also founded the camp of Klondike between Tonopah and Goldfield, and he supplied financial backing to help the Rawhide district get started. True to the code of the prospector, he repaid his benefactors generously: Ford got $25,000 in good mining stock for his grubstake, and Judge Powers was given $10,000 worth of securities.[1]

Jack Davis found himself, for the first time in his life, a capitalist and a man with rich and powerful business associates. George Nixon, whose $1,500 grubstake had earned him a $50,000 return, was now a United States Senator and closely associated with Davis in several ventures. George Wingfield, perhaps the biggest operator in the entire Goldfield camp and later to become the kingmaker of Nevada politics as well as the creator of the great Goldfield Consolidated Mines, was also associated with Davis. When the Diamondfield Triangle Gold Mining Company was formed with a capitalization of one million dollars, Jack Davis became president and George Wingfield was vice-president

An advertisement for Jack's Diamondfield Triangle Gold Mining Company.

Nothing remains today of the tiny town of Diamondfield, Nevada, named after Jack Davis. (From *Western World*, April 1905; courtesy of Denver Public Library Western Collection)

and treasurer. When the Diamondfield Bullfrog Mining Company was organized, United States Senator Tasker L. Oddie—the original owner of the Tonopah discovery—was named president of the company, with Diamondfield Jack as vice-president.

In the creation of each of these companies Jack Davis showed his gratitude by naming as corporate secretary Willis Sears, one of the two men who had ridden with a reprieve from Minidoka to Albion to save him from the gallows in 1901. Sears had come to Nevada to be a partner of Davis in the townsite company of Diamondfield, and had been given an interest in several mines. The other Idaho cowboy who had ridden with Sears, Charley Krise, also came to Diamondfield and was given a lease on the Quartzite claim —one of Jack's best properties. So Jack Davis built something of a reputation as a man who paid back those who had helped him.

He also rebuilt his reputation as a gunman. When the Western Federation of Miners and the Wobblies were stirring up considerable labor unrest in Goldfield in 1906 and 1907, a handful of tough mineowners including Davis were the only men willing to stand up to the unions. During the newspaper strike Davis and Wingfield bought newspapers from a street vendor, knocked down two men who called them "scabs," and with guns drawn stood alongside the newsboy defying the hostile crowd. On another occasion Diamondfield Jack stood off a mob of 150 men in a demonstration of courage that would have impressed even his harshest critics in Idaho. The men were pursuing a nonunion

[161]

miner through the streets, while the sheriff stood by, doing nothing to intervene. The man escaped into the office of George Nixon, while Diamondfield Jack stood outside with drawn guns daring any of the men to cross a line he had scratched in the dust. No one crossed the line, and no harm came to the miner.

A few days later two union men, charged with killing a restaurant owner who had hired "scab" help, were about to be hanged by a committee of twenty-five vigilantes, while the sheriff and constable again stood by doing nothing. Even though he was fanatically opposed to the union miners, Davis—perhaps remembering his own close encounter with the noose— singlehandedly stopped the lynching. The two men were ultimately tried and convicted at Hawthorne, Nevada, a few months later. In an interesting sidelight to this trial, one witness testified that the IWW had marked both the restaurant owner and Diamondfield Jack for assassination.

During the height of the union terrorism in Goldfield in 1907 Diamondfield Jack happened upon two men who were shooting at John S. Cook, a prominent local banker who was associated with Davis in the Diamondfield Mining Company. Davis returned the fire, drove the men off, and discovered that they had been saturating the MacKenzie building with coal oil when Cook had interrupted them.[2]

Out of his involvement in these many incidents Diamondfield Jack became a local legend—referred to variously as "the most notorious gunman in camp" and as a "walking arsenal." One newspaper man claimed he saw Davis so heavily armed that he was unable to get up from a chair without help. Clearly, Diamondfield Jack played more than a minor role in the battle between the unions and the mineowners in Goldfield. Ironically, by the time Governor Sparks finally got federal troops into town to suppress the trouble, things had calmed down considerably, and the camp was already starting the inevitable decline that comes to all boom towns. But while Goldfield proved to be a death blow for John Sparks, it marked the zenith of Diamondfield Jack Davis' career in terms of wealth and respectability.

Some authors have implied that Diamondfield Jack was merely a hired gunman during this period, but contemporary accounts seem to suggest that he was no longer a hireling in any sense. His name was mentioned frequently in association with, and as an equal to, the members of the Goldfield elite: Nixon, Oddie, Wingfield, Cook, *et al.* A national magazine credited him with being one of the four founders of the protective association which ultimately defeated the miners' union strike. This same magazine implied that Davis was just a step below the tycoon ranks when it reported:

The two Georges [Nixon and Wingfield] now control a $50,000,000 corporation of consolidated mines with "Diamondfield" Jack Davis of Idaho, Utah, Montana, and Colorado as one of their right hand men.

This particular article, entitled "Pluck and Luck in the Desert," was billed as "a glance at the careers of the foremost men in that little company of rugged pioneers

who established Goldfield on the map of Nevada." It
devoted all of its space to just two men: George Wingfield and Diamondfield Jack Davis. It concluded:

> Nevertheless the fact remains that these two quiet, steady-
> eyed young men have passed through many desperate mo-
> ments that required the sort of nerve and fibre of which epic
> heroes are made; and undoubtedly if there were more of
> their calibre down in the new county seat of Esmeralda there
> would have been no demand on the government for regi-
> ments of regulars to settle Goldfield's labor troubles.[3]

Perhaps the highlight of the article's treatment of
Davis is a description of his introduction to former-
Governor Hunt of Idaho, the man who had pardoned
him in 1902. The two men had never met, so when
they chanced to be in the exclusive Montezuma Club
in Goldfield at the same time they were introduced by
Henry Weber, one of the new millionaires of the district. The conversation was hardly animated and natural; each man was cautious about reopening what was
obviously an old wound. Hunt's remarks indicated that
he mistakenly associated Diamondfield Jack's imprisonment and pardon with the Coeur d'Alene troubles—
which may have been natural if the onetime governor
attributed his own political defeat to public reaction
to his pardon policies, which had been exercised largely
in behalf of Coeur d'Alene miners. Davis, too, found
it difficult to warm up to a conversation with a man
whose slowness and ineptness had kept him imprisoned
for two years. But eventually the atmosphere thawed,
and when Davis mentioned the fact that he still had

the hangman's rope as a souvenir, the governor's curiosity got the best of him and the two men left the club together to inspect the trophy they had both helped to create.

Jack Davis was a somebody at last—the kind of celebrity to whom curious visitors wanted to be introduced. He was well known in many camps, and was featured several times by national magazines in articles describing life in this last great mining boom of the West. In one particularly purple passage a writer in *Cosmopolitan Magazine* described how Judge Powers had

. . . grubstaked Diamondfield Jack to a burro and a month's food, put his hand on his shoulder, asked the God of the friendless and the evilly used to stand by him, and sent him out of his sight and his memory as one sends a stray dog into the night after giving him a bone and patting him on his shaggy head.

Diamondfield Jack went straight into the gleaming silver of the desert—and found gold, rich, crumbling, placer-gold, and—be it stated for the benefit of all skeptics—he sent the lawyer who had given him a chance for his life shares enough in the mines he found to keep him rich the rest of his life.[4]

This writer ended by quoting Diamondfield Jack on the subject of Goldfield: "A man with a little capital can be a Croesus here in a few weeks." While Diamondfield Jack may have been speaking from personal experience, he was also speaking as a mining promoter who at that moment was trying to sell a big block of stock in the Diamondfield Triangle Company at fifteen cents a share to any would-be Croesus who wanted to buy.

Davis himself became something of a master of the superlative expression, as witnessed by the advertisements for his Davis-Wheeler Company. When the Wonder district of central Nevada was opened, the company's advertisement in the *Goldfield News* headlined:

WILL YOU FOLLOW HIM IN WONDER?
DIAMONDFIELD JACK DAVIS—
THE MAN WITHOUT A FAILURE

More modest type proclaimed:

Known throughout Nevada and the United States at large as one of the most successful operators in the mining world today. Those who have followed him have made fortunes. He is the owner of and has developed more producing mines than any other one man in Nevada.[5]

Even though Davis was responsible for this glowing account of his own ability, it was apparent that he did, indeed, have a strong reputation as a successful developer of mining properties. Other companies used the magic lure of his name to attract investors to their nearby properties, and a newspaper account of Jack Davis' presence in a mining community often created considerable speculation and excitement around the area.

It would be a mistake to assume, however, that Diamondfield Jack was a universally-respected and solid citizen of the mining camps. His name appeared from time to time in the local papers in connection with disturbances of the peace, as well as in the mining news. In addition to his encounters with the Wobblies in Goldfield, he had a fracas with a deputy sheriff in Rawhide and a run-in with claim-jumpers in Bullfrog. He was too blunt and aggressive to be accepted by the new social aristocrats of Goldfield. For example, the *Goldfield Review,* in describing another man named Davis, said, "He is not related to 'Diamondfield Jack' Davis. He is another type of man, a gentleman every inch." Yet, at the same time, Diamondfield Jack was equally unacceptable to the rank and file of miners and camp followers, who distrusted and feared him.

Jack Davis even became a bit touchy about the way people were reacting to him. In October of 1908 the *Saturday Evening Post* ran a short story with a Goldfield setting which particularly annoyed the hot-tempered promoter. The story, written by James Hopper and entitled "The Embarrassing Conduct of Benjamin Ellis, Millionaire," described how a tenderfoot millionaire went out into the desert with a local character named Diamond Jack. A few days later Diamond Jack returned alone, loaded with money. Still later the body of the murdered Mr. Ellis was discovered, and Diamond Jack was charged with the murder.[6]

The real Diamondfield Jack probably had good reason to be unhappy with the story. The author's descriptions of Diamond Jack resembled closely the real man —"dark and slight and indescribably impudent"— and the characterization of Diamond Jack as "the idealized Western villain of a Broadway melodrama" seemed remarkably similar to that of the character who has emerged through the preceding pages of this book. The author reinforced the similarity when he described the trial: witnesses testified how, after Ellis' disappearance, Diamond Jack spent money lavishly in a saloon and boasted of how he was able to "milk dollars out of tenderfeet." However, another man supplied testimony that raised reasonable doubt about Diamond Jack's guilt, so the jury eventually turned him loose. That same night Diamond Jack celebrated his acquittal by getting gloriously drunk in a Goldfield saloon, and ultimately boasting of how he really did kill the millionaire. The story ended as a small group of citizens quietly escorted the boisterous gunman out of the saloon—and lynched him.

To a person familiar with the legendary mining man in Goldfield, the character of Diamond Jack in the story certainly seemed to be patterned after Diamondfield Jack. Davis was angry enough to try legal action, instead of the direct action of "cutting it in smoke." As the *Rhyolite Daily Bulletin* noted:

Diamondfield Jack Davis has sued the Saturday Evening Post for $250,000 damages for defamation of character. Holy smoke, how that sheep herder [*sic!*] has grown in value (in his own estimation), during the last few years.[7]

The ultimate outcome of the lawsuit apparently has not been recorded, but the entire episode stands as another interesting milestone in the man's life—the point at which he was, for the first time, offended by the very notoriety in which he had previously gloried.

Thus, the palmy days of the Goldfield boom had the effect of making Jack Davis, at least momentarily, a wealthy and famous man. But they had one other effect on him as well—a personal one. Here, in 1906, he met the great love of his life, Diamond Tooth Lil. Born Evelyn Fiala in Vienna, Lil was a onetime dance-hall girl with entrepreneurial talent who ran dance halls and "rooming houses" all over the West. Lil was in Goldfield for only about a year during the height of the boom, but she hit it off famously with the gunman-turned-capitalist during this time. Jack Davis had remarried in Tonopah in 1904, and his new wife was with him in Goldfield, but this circumstance did not seem to interfere with the relationship between Jack and Lil. Lil may have had a husband at the time, too; she had nine of them during her long and colorful career.[8]

The diamond, and her nickname, came shortly after Lil left Goldfield. In Reno she won a horse-racing bet with a local dentist. The tooth, which became her trademark, was created for her by the dentist in payment of the bet—a right front gold tooth in which was centered a diamond of about one third carat.

Even though they rarely saw each other afterward, Diamondfield Jack and Diamond Tooth Lil in a short year had developed a lasting affinity for each other. They were from the same mold—sporting, brash, flamboyant, and tough. They epitomized the Nevada mining camps—the Goldfield of Tex Rickard and the Gans-Nelson fight, the Rawhide of Herman Knickerbocker's immortal eulogy on "Riley Grannan's Last Adventure." Rarely in the pages of Western history do we see a couple quite like Diamondfield Jack and Diamond Tooth Lil.

If Jack Davis' meteoric rise to fame from 1903 to 1907 seems a strange contrast to the obscurity of his early life, so does his drift back into obscurity in later years seem a strange reversal of fate for a man whose Goldfield associates were senators, bankers, and important mining men. After 1908 the trail of Diamondfield Jack becomes dim once again, and only infrequent newspaper items report his coming and going around the Western mining camps. In 1909 the Goldfield papers reported the divorce proceedings which Mrs. Davis initiated against her husband, charging desertion and cruelty. That same year the papers also reported that a local resident had run into Davis and Cook, the one-time Goldfield banker, in Guaymas, Mexico. The two men had reported that they were then mining in the province of Sonora where they had a "good thing" going for them. The following year the *Los Angeles Times,* in reporting the return of Davis from the west coast of Mexico, fancifully described how the mining man had been engaged in a losing gun battle with a large number of Yaqui Indians for several days when finally the chief recognized Davis as an old friend and called off his braves.

In 1913 Davis turned up in Butte, Montana, where he became involved in an altercation with three IWW men who threatened him at gun point. Davis pulled a knife, and managed to slash two of his assailants before a shot caught him in the chin. A Reno newspaper headlined, "Diamondfield Jack Davis May Die of Wounds," but a bit of quick first-aid was all that he actually required. He was then escorted out of town—

for his own protection—by the Butte police. Eventually he reached Salt Lake City where he was patched up with a dental plate that became another battle scar to be displayed proudly by the gunman.

In commenting on the indestructibility of Diamondfield Jack, newspaper accounts of his 1913 escapade in Butte pointed out that earlier that year he had been reported shot by a Mexican firing squad for meddling in the revolution there. Later, he had turned up alive but broke in New York City. Although factual details are lacking, several brief accounts of Davis' life do mention his connection with the Díaz-Huerta-Madero revolution in Mexico. It is interesting to recall that fifteen years earlier, as he sat in the Cassia County jail, Davis had talked about leading a revolution in Mexico, and dividing the country with President Díaz!

Another undocumented assertion, occurring in several accounts, is that Davis' father died in Brazil, leaving twelve million dollars to his second wife and his family. Diamondfield Jack was supposed to have received one million dollars from the estate, but evidences of this money—a sizeable and conspicuous fortune in those days—were apparently never detected by southwestern newsmen, who continued to mention Davis from time to time. Thus, it seems likely that the million dollars never really existed.

Very little is known of Diamondfield Jack during the next twenty years. In 1919 a Reno newspaper reported that Davis was back from Mexico, adding the magic of his name to the promotion of the Divide mining district near Tonopah. A wire-service story from

Fresno in 1927 reported that Davis was then living on a claim in the Spring Mountains west of Las Vegas. In 1935 he was reportedly in on a short-lived mining boom at Oasis, California, in Fish Lake Valley.

In 1937 the Goldfield paper reported that Jack Davis was back in town, visiting old friends and talking of building a new mill on his old Daisy claim. In 1938 the *Los Angeles Times* carried a lengthy story describing a visit by Davis to Frank Jordan, California Secretary of State, in Sacramento. According to this account, Davis brought tungsten ore with him to Sacramento, ore which he had mined on claims in the Sierras and in Nevada.

The 1930's had been lean years for American mining men, but World War II caused a general improvement in the mining picture. Tungsten ore notwithstanding, Jack Davis did not seem to share in the better fortunes of most mining men, however. In 1943 he was back in Sacramento, looking for a grubstake to develop a find he claimed to have made in Amador County, California. Frank Jordan found him a grubstake, the money being furnished by Dr. J. F. Peattie, the chief surgeon of the Tidewater Oil Company. But neither Jordan nor Peattie ever saw any more of Davis or the money.[9]

In 1945 Diamondfield Jack and Diamond Tooth Lil found each other again. In a colorful reunion in a Las Vegas casino the two quaint characters talked of the "good old days" in Goldfield, and consumed enormous quantities of champagne while telling each other what had been happening since that time. After the reunion Lil returned to Long Beach, California, where she had been living, and Jack soon followed her there. In 1946 John MacLane, who was writing a biography of James Hawley, wrote to Lil, asking what she knew of Diamondfield Jack. Part of her colorful and candid answer follows:

> In regards to Jack he s been bothering me early mornings around 6 A.M. . . . He is all in cant hardly breed. So I havend seen him since, he has no address. As he moves so much. He owes me a few dollars, wich I dont care, and he is so mean, uses bad language and he wont give me no decent answer so am glad he is gone there is no way I can find out were he lives, as he talks foolish. You know he must be real old.[10]

Certainly the Diamondfield Jack Davis of the early 1940's—bypassed in the prosperity of the war, bumming money from friends, aimlessly wandering from place to place—was a sorry figure when compared to the Goldfield tycoon he once had been. But he never lost the optimism of the prospector, and he continued to dream of striking it rich once again. Late in 1948 he was back in the desert, prospecting in the vicinity of Goodsprings, Nevada. Mrs. Celesta Lowe, who ran the hotel in that community, encountered Davis late one evening, when he irately demanded T-bone steaks after the restaurant was closed. Cantankerous as ever, he announced that he was there to open one of the old mines in the district, but that because of Mrs. Lowe's refusal to serve him, he would also build a new cafe to put the Lowe establishment out of business![11]

This was the last recorded encounter that anyone had with Davis out in the mining districts. At this time he was apparently living in Las Vegas, and reportedly working as a shill in a gambling casino. The *Las Vegas Review-Journal* had been trying to get details of his life in order to do a feature story on the colorful prospector, but Diamondfield Jack had been reluctant to cooperate with the newspaper. Instead, he hoped that he might replenish his money by selling his life story to an author. He agreed to pose for a picture for the newspaper, but the picture was never taken, for a few days later, on December 28, 1948, Jack Davis had an unlikely accident.

Stepping from the curb into a downtown Las Vegas street, Diamondfield Jack was struck by a taxicab which was backing up along the curb. He was taken immediately to a hospital, where his condition did not appear to be serious. He absolved the cab driver of blame, saying, "I was just not looking where I was going." From his hospital bed a day or so later he was quoted as saying that he was reforming in his old age: "Yes sir, I'm quitting whiskey and smoking. I'll live to be a hundred. I'll be out of here in a few days."

It was a brave—and typical—assertion. But it did not come true. On January 2, 1949, Diamondfield Jack died in the Clark County General Hospital.

His obituary in the *Las Vegas Review-Journal* explained how the paper had been trying to find out more about the "self-styled last of the western badmen" at the time of his death. It also reported some of the high spots of his career, but the facts of the story were of necessity incomplete and inaccurate. For example, the paper had this to say about how Davis was released from prison in Idaho:

> He [Davis] had supreme confidence that the governor would intervene, insisting the chief executive was a silent partner in a cattle-rustling venture which had netted thousands of dollars. Nobody ever knew whether this was one of Davis' yarns or was true. But the fact remains he was pardoned at the last possible moment and walked out of the prison a free man.
>
> Some of his biographers hold to the theory that "Diamondfield" virtually blasted the pardon loose when he revealed to the guards that the chemicals he had asked them to bring him had finally been compounded into TNT, and he was ready to blow the whole prison to bits if he wasn't freed.[12]

The *Tonopah Times-Bonanza* was less speculative in its obituary. It conceded that Davis was "an enigma even to his closest friends," and admitted that even though he had a lurid reputation, very little was actually known about the man, whom it described as reticent and quiet.

The newspapers were not alone in their inability to provide factual information about the man's life. Even the official death certificate for Jackson Lee Davis contained questionable information with respect to his age, which was given as eighty-five.[13] A safe presumption would seem to be that—lacking direct documentary evidence—a man would normally have better knowledge of his own age than would his friends. Diamondfield Jack Davis had given his age to the Idaho Board of Pardons years before: 1870 would have been his birthdate, according to that statement. This would mean that he was seventy-eight, rather than eighty-five, when he died in Las Vegas.

But herein lies the mystery of the man. He was such a consummate liar, such a stretcher of the truth, that even the facts of his own life as he related them cannot be trusted. For example, late in his life he told author John MacLane that he had served in the Bolivian Army —as a general, no less—in 1878. By the chronology he had established before the Board of Pardons, this would have made him eight years old at the time of this interesting experience!

After Diamondfield Jack's death in 1949 only one survivor remained of the colorful group of people who were his Idaho and Nevada contemporaries. That person was Diamond Tooth Lil, the Goldfield dance hall queen. When she died in a rest home in California in 1967 the wire services called her a "legend of the West." Significantly, the Associated Press found it necessary to use the name of Diamondfield Jack in establishing her credentials for that title:

> As a showgirl and hotel operator she counted some of the most notorious gamblers and gun slingers among her friends, including convicted murderer Diamondfield Jack Davis—who became one of her nine husbands.[14]

With the last of his cronies dead, this wire service account—inaccurate as it may be with respect to any marriage between Jack and Lil—marked the end of Diamondfield Jack's notoriety. Even the sequel to the

[176]

story of Jackson Lee Davis was ended. It ended with the same mystery and notoriety which characterized the entire story of his life. If it has been difficult to separate fact from fiction, the blame must go to Diamondfield Jack himself, a man who never worried a great deal about the distinction between the two.

NOTES

[1]Facts concerning Davis' mining ventures are reconstructed largely from magazine articles, and from the clippings and newspaper files of the Nevada Historical Society. The claim-jumping episode is mentioned by C. B. Glasscock in *Gold in Them Hills,* and is confirmed by Mrs. Charlotte Nay, onetime Goldfield resident, in a letter to Mrs. Myrtle Myles of the Nevada Historical Society. Details of the grubstake appear in *Western World* for April, 1905.

[2]Stories of violence in Goldfield appear in several accounts. The best documentation is in Laura A. White, "History of the Labor Struggles in Goldfield, Nevada," an unpublished M.A. thesis at the University of Nebraska, 1912.

[3]Barton W. Currie, "Pluck and Luck in the Desert," *Harpers Weekly,* April 11, 1908, pp. 28–29.

[4]Winifred Black, "Gold of the Burning Desert," *Cosmopolitan,* September, 1905, p. 524.

[5]*Goldfield News,* December 8, 1906.

[6]James Hopper, "The Embarrassing Conduct of Benjamin Ellis, Millionaire," *Saturday Evening Post,* October 24, 1908, p. 3.

[7]*Rhyolite Daily Bulletin,* November 14, 1908.

[8]Diamond Tooth Lil is described in several feature stories in the *Idaho Statesman.* She was well known in Boise where she ran a "rooming house" for a number of years. Fred and Jo Mazzulla in *Brass Checks and Red Lights* devote two pages to Diamond Tooth Lil, including several pictures.

[9]The story from Sacramento has been widely quoted in newspaper accounts, but in 1962 Frank Jordan told the author that he knew nothing of Davis' life prior to his coming to California. The grubstake transaction is described in letters to the author from Frank Jordan and from Yvonne Peattie, daughter of Dr. Peattie.

[10]Lil's letter is quoted in MacLane, pp. 119–121.

[11]Mrs. Celesta Lowe describes the experience in Goodsprings in a letter to the author dated July 15, 1965.

[12]*Las Vegas Review-Journal,* January 3, 1949.

[13]According to the University of Nevada Library, the death certificate for Davis is filed with the Nevada State Registrar of Vital Statistics.

[14]Associated Press dispatch appearing in the *Reno Evening Gazette,* September 8, 1967.

Bibliography

I. Unpublished Materials

Transcript of *State* v. *Davis,* on file with the Clerk of the Idaho Supreme Court, Boise.

Transcript of *State* v. *Gray,* in the Hawley papers of the Idaho Historical Society.

Affidavits, depositions, correspondence, scrapbooks, and other papers pertaining to the Davis case in the Hawley papers, Idaho Historical Society, Boise.

Portions of the transcript and correspondence pertaining to the Davis case in the Borah papers, Idaho Historical Society, Boise.

Lewis, Albert L., "Sagebrush Rhetoric: The Oratory of James H. Hawley," unpublished Ph.D. dissertation, University of Oregon, 1967.

White, Laura A., "History of the Labor Struggles in Goldfield, Nevada," unpublished M.A. thesis, University of Nebraska, 1912.

II. Court Cases

State v. *Davis,* 53 Pacific 678.
In re Davis, 59 Pacific 544.

[179]

State v. *Davis,* 65 Pacific 429.
State v. *Davis,* 66 Pacific 932.
Sweet v. *Ballentine,* 69 Pacific 995.
State v. *Davis,* 8 Idaho 115.
Davis v. *Burke,* 38 CCA 299.
Davis v. *Burke,* 97 Fed. Rep. 501.
Davis v. *Burke,* 179 US 339.

III.   Newspapers

Albion *Cassia County Times,* 1897, 1898.
Boise *Evening Capital News,* 1900, 1901, 1902.
Boise *Idaho Statesman,* 1897, 1898, 1900, 1901, 1902, 1938, 1945, 1949, 1963.
Caldwell Tribune, 1892.
Goldfield News, 1905, 1906, 1907, 1909, (*and Weekly Tribune*), 1937.
Goldfield Review, 1908.
Goldfield Tribune, 1910.
Las Vegas Review-Journal, 1948, 1949, 1967.
Los Angeles Times, 1910, 1938.
Rawhide Rustler, 1908.
Reno Evening Gazette, 1967.
Reno *Nevada State Journal,* 1913, 1919.
Rhyolite Daily Bulletin, 1908.
Tonopah Sun, 1905.
Tonopah Times-Bonanza, 1949.

IV.   Books

Beale, Merrill D. and Wells, Merle. *History of Idaho.* New York: Lewis Publishing Co., 1959.

Elliott, Russell R. *Nevada's Twentieth-Century Mining Boom: Tonopah, Goldfield, Ely.* Reno: University of Nevada Press, 1966.

French, Hiram T. *History of Idaho.* Chicago: Lewis Publishing Co., 1914.

Bibliography

Glasscock, C. B. *Gold in Them Hills.* New York: Grosset & Dunlap, 1940.

Grover, David H. *Debaters and Dynamiters: The Story of the Haywood Trial.* Corvallis: Oregon State University Press, 1964.

Hobson, C. C., editor. *The Idaho Digest and Blue Book.* Caldwell, Idaho: The Caxton Printers, 1935.

Idaho Historical Society. *Idaho, A Brief History.* Boise: Idaho Historical Society, 1962.

Lillard, Richard G. *Desert Challenge.* New York: Alfred Knopf, 1949.

MacLane, John. *A Sagebrush Lawyer.* New York: Pandick Press, 1953.

Mazzulla, Fred and Jo. *Brass Checks and Red Lights.* Denver: Fred Mazzulla, 1967.

McKenna, Marian C. *Borah.* Ann Arbor: University of Michigan Press, 1961.

Murbarger, Nell. *Ghosts of the Glory Trail.* Palm Desert, California: Desert Magazine Press, 1956.

Myrick, David. *Railroads of Nevada and Eastern California.* Vol. II. Berkeley, California: Howell North Books, 1963.

Pound, Roscoe. *Organization of Courts.* Boston: Little, Brown & Company, 1940.

Robertson, Frank C. and Harris, Beth Kay. *Boom Towns of the Great Basin.* Denver: Sage Books, 1962.

Walgamott, Charles S. *Six Decades Back.* Caldwell, Idaho: The Caxton Printers, 1936.

Wentworth, Edward. *America's Sheep Trails.* Ames: Iowa State University Press, 1948.

Who Was Who in America. Vol. I, 1897–1942. Chicago: A. N. Marquis Co., 1942.

W. P. A. Writers' Project. *Idaho Lore.* Caldwell, Idaho: The Caxton Printers, 1939.

V. Magazine Articles

Black, Winifred. "Gold of the Burning Desert," *Cosmopolitan,* September, 1905.

Carr, Harry C. "The Nevada Goldfields," *Collier's,* July 29, 1905.

Currie, Barton W. "How the West Dealt with One Labor Union," *Harpers Weekley,* June 22, 1907.

.... "Pluck and Luck in the Desert," *Harpers Weekley,* April 11, 1908.

Connolly, C. P. "Presidential Possibilities: Borah of Idaho," *Collier's,* July 31, 1915.

" 'Diamondfield' Jack Davis," *Successful American,* August, 1906.

"Founder of Town in Nevada," *Western World,* April, 1905.

Fulton, R. L. "Camp Life on a Great Cattle Range in Northern Nevada," *Sunset,* July, 1900.

Grover, David H. "Diamondfield Jack: A Range War in Court," *Idaho Yesterdays,* Summer, 1963.

.... "James H. Hawley, Pioneer Persuader and Pragmatist," *Western Speech,* Winter, 1966.

Hopper, James. "The Embarrassing Conduct of Benjamin Ellis, Millionaire," *Saturday Evening Post,* October 24, 1908.

Tondel, Frank P. "As I Remember Goldfield," *Nevada Historical Society Quarterly,* July–September, 1960.

Index

Index

Index

Index

Minidoka, Idaho, 103, 132–134, 161
Moore, C. B., 32, 56
Moore, George T., 46, 65–66
Mormon Church (Latter Day Saints), 13, 36, 41–43, 43n, 101, 116–117, 150
Morrison, John T., 133
Motion for retrial, 71–72

Nampa, Idaho, 36
Natatorium resort, 146–147
Nevada Historical Society, 4
New York City, 171
Nixon, George, 159–160, 162–163
Norton, A. D., 10–11, 15, 92, 102, 108, 137, 140

Oakley, Idaho, 16, 17, 19, 27–28, 51, 54, 115–116
Oasis, California, 172
Oddie, T. L., 161, 163
Ogden, Utah, 102, 134, 138, 140
Oregon Short Line Railroad, 10, 103, 123
Oregon Trail, 9–10, 43
Orr, William, 18, 48
"Outside" men, 16, 24, 26–27
Owyhee County, Idaho, 8

Pardon of Diamondfield Jack, 143–146
Patrie, Mark, 119
Peattie, Dr. J. F., 172
Perkins, Harvey L., 28, 46–47
Perky, Kirtland I., 42, 56–60, 63–65, 69, 76–77, 79, 84, 97, 101, 122–123, 130, 156
Pierce, J. M., 78
Pierson, W. E., 30
Point ranch, 25, 54, 67, 69, 79, 83, 90, 137, 154

Politics in Idaho, 99–100, 115–116, 132–133, 150
Populist party, 100, 116
Porter, George, 34, 51
Powers, Orlando W., 42, 56, 57–59, 121–122, 130, 134, 138, 156, 160, 165
Promontory, Utah, 10
Puckett, Will, 42, 63, 91, 103–104, 130

Quinn, William, 30
Quarles, Justice, 131

Raft River, 10, 46
Rawhide, Nevada, 160, 167, 169
Redke, Frank, 116
Reno, Nevada, 32, 84, 90, 137, 157, 169–171
Republican party, 100, 116, 119, 133, 150
Rewards for capture of Davis, 35, 37–38, 94
Rhodes, Cecil, 8
Rhyolite Daily Bulletin, 168
Rice, Buck, 15, 54, 86, 91–92, 102, 108, 137, 140, 154
Rickard, Tex, 169
Roberts, Dr. R. D., 55
Robinson, I. T., 54, 93, 108
Robinson, Mrs. Lou, 66, 69-70
Robinson, M. G., 10
Rock Creek, 9–10, 83–86
Rogers, John C., 42, 45–46, 56–59, 65–66, 69–70, 108, 121, 130, 134, 138, 157
Roosevelt, Theodore, 133, 157
Rowberry, George P., 67–68

Sacramento, California, 172
Salmon Falls River, 11, 13, 23, 71, 83–84, 153

Index

Salt Lake City, Utah, 36, 42, 156, 171
Sandow (horse), 24, 31
San Francisco, California, 11, 40, 136
San Jacinto ranch, 23, 49–51
San Juan mining district, 9
Santa Rosa, California, 38
Saturday Evening Post, 167–168
Schmidt, E. H., 46
Sears, Hardy, 78, 115
Sears, Willis, 124, 161
Severe, Edgar, 27, 47–48
Shawnee, Oklahoma, 37
Sheep industry, 12–13, 149, 152–153
Sheep wagon, 28–29
Shoe Sole ranch, 11–12, 15, 32, 55
Shoshone Basin, 11, 19, 35, 48, 83, 85, 87, 122
Short, Thomas, 79
Silver City, Idaho, 8
Silver issue in Idaho, 100, 116, 133
Smith, Frank, 24, 32, 34–35, 38, 49–52, 55–57, 65, 69–70, 77, 79
Snake River, 9–10, 13, 85, 124, 153
Soloman, Louis, 107
Sonora, Mexico, 8, 170
Spanish-American War, 113
Sparks-Harrell Cattle Co., 3, 7, 15–16, 19–20, 23–24, 31–34, 37–38, 49, 55–56, 77, 83–85, 92, 96, 130, 136, 153
Sparks, John, 11–16, 32, 38, 40, 77, 101–102, 107–108, 130, 132–136, 140, 143, 145, 150, 157, 158*n*, 163
Speed of horses, estimates of, 49–51, 56

Spring Mountains of Nevada, 172
St. Cyr., W. S., 117
Steunenberg, C. B., 73
Steunenberg, Frank, 73, 95–97, 99–100, 113, 119, 132, 155
Stewart, Judge, 119–121
Stockslager, C. O., 42, 59–60, 71, 74, 108–109, 116, 120, 131, 150–151
Story, Dr. R. T., 28–30, 47
Streeter, Randolph, 33, 78–79, 93
Sublette Cut-off, 9–10
Summation speeches in Davis trial, 57–59
Sunset Magazine, 130
Surveyor, testimony of, 52
Suspects, arrest of, 37–38
Swan, A. H., 15
Sweetser, Lewis, 78

Tatro, J. F., 90
Testimony in Davis case, 46–57
Test rides, 67–71, 119
Thomas, Eva, 84
Tinnin, John, 11–13
Tolman, Bill, 17–20, 23, 35, 51, 100
Tonopah, Nevada, 148, 159–161, 169
Tonopah Times-Bonanza, 175
Tranmer, Harve, 24, 26, 31, 49, 52–53, 73
Transcript of Davis case, 72–74
Trial: of Jack Davis, 42–43, 45–60; of Fred Gleason, 63–64; of Jeff Gray, 107–110
Trotter, Bill, 9, 49
Tungsten ore, 172
Twin Falls, Idaho, 9
Twin Falls County, 153, 157
Two Mile Limit, 12

Index